CW01023830

WIRELESS TELEGRAPHY;

ITS ORIGINS, DEVELOPMENT, INVENTIONS, AND APPARATUS

BY

CHARLES HENRY SEWALL

AUTHOR OF " PATENTED TELEPHONY," "THE FUTURE OF LONG-DISTANCE COMMUNICATION "

WITH 85 DIAGRAMS AND ILLUSTRATIONS

SECOND EDITION CORRECTED.

REESE LIBRARY
OF THE
UNIVERSITY
OF
CALIFORNIA

NEW YORK

D. VAN NOSTRAND COMPANY

23 MURRAY AND 27 WARREN STS.

1904

TK 5741
55

REESE

COPYRIGHT, 1903, BY

D. VAN NOSTRAND COMPANY

Printing Statement:

Due to the very old age and scarcity of this book,
many of the pages may be hard to read due to the
blurring of the original text, possible missing pages,
missing text, dark backgrounds and other issues
beyond our control.

Because this is such an important and rare work, we
believe it is best to reproduce this book regardless of
its original condition.

Thank you for your understanding.

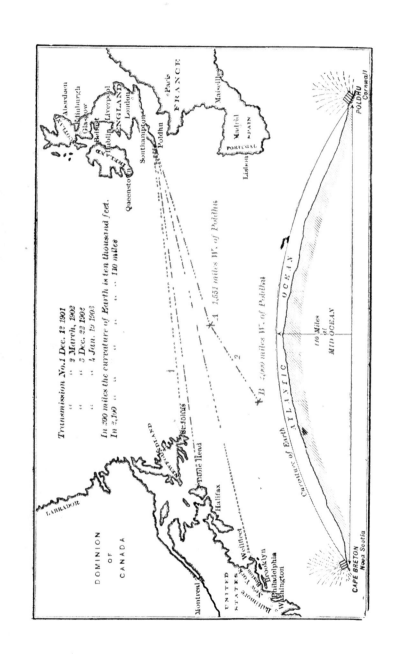

PREFACE

THE aim of this book is to present a comprehensive view of wireless telegraphy, its history, principles, systems, and possibilities in theory and practice. In considering inventions controversy has been avoided, although the claims of individual inventors have been carefully defined. Because of the complexity of the subject a certain amount of allusion in one part, to matters dealt with in another, has been inevitable; but it is hoped that such repetition may prove helpful to the reader. The book itself is designed to be of use both to the general public and to the technical student.

The author begs to acknowledge to the publishers his obligation for kind co-operation; to the *Century Magazine* for extracts from the article by Mr. McGrath of St. Johns; and to the *Scientific American* for extracts and diagrams from an article by Mr. A. F. Collins.

CHARLES H. SEWALL.

NEW YORK, September, 1903.

196526

IN FRONTISPIECE, the repetition in No. 1 of the group of three dots, S, illustrates the stream of signals that were sent out from Poldhu, England, and which Marconi heard in the telephone at Cape Race, Newfoundland. Three short marks combined with a longer one, as shown in No. 2, represent the code designation for the letter V, a favorite experimenting signal with wireless-telegraph workers. The dots and dashes in No. 3, from Table-Head, say in the alphabet of the European telegraphs "first msg (message) shore to shore"; and in line No. 4 from Wellfleet, Massachusetts, to Poldhu are Morse characters, such as are used by American telegraphers, arranged to spell "Roosevelt to Edward."

TABLE OF CONTENTS.

PART I.

PART II.

PART III.

PART IV.

WIRELESS TELEGRAPHY.

PART I.

PROPHECY.

"Canst thou send lightnings, that they may go, and say unto thee, 'Here we are?'" — JOB, 38th chapter, 35th verse.

IN 1632 Galileo wrote a dialogue of which a Latin translation appeared at Leyden in 1700. Mr. Robert Sabine, in his work on the *Electric Telegraph*,[1] rendered into English a paragraph from the Latin version, wherein Sagredus, one of the colloquists, is made to say:

"You remind me of one who offered to sell me a secret art, by which through the attraction of a certain magnet needle it would be possible to converse across a space of two or three thousand miles. And I said to him that I would willingly become the purchaser provided only that I might first make a trial of the art, and that it would be sufficient for the purpose if I were to place myself in one corner of the sofa and he in the other. He replied that in so short a distance the action would be scarcely discernible: so I dismissed the fellow, and said that it was not convenient for me just then to travel into Egypt or Muscovy for the purpose of trying the experiment, but that if he chose to go there himself I would remain in Venice and attend to the rest."

In the sixties of the nineteenth century Mr. Sabine supposed this expression to be a prescient description of telegraphy with wires. In 1877 it could be better associ-

---

[1] D. Van Nostrand, New York, 1869.

I

ated with telephone transmission over a conductor. To-day, however, we can readily see that Galileo wrote of "Wireless Telephony," an art not quite arrived. It will be observed that as translated the words are "to converse," not "to signal"; and the correctness in translation is corroborated by the fact of the action at short distance being undiscernible. Readers of this generation will understand that between two persons sitting upon the same sofa, telephonic action is not palpable; whereas nearness of sender and receiver is no bar to the observation of signals.

It may be that Galileo had read the "Prolusiones Academicae" of Strada, published in 1617, and which described communication at a distance by means of two needles that had been touched with lodestone. These needles were mounted upon pivots. If either of them were moved it caused its mate to turn and to point in the same direction as itself. Possibly Galileo had an independent vision of wireless communication, seeing farther than Strada, and dared make of it but guarded mention. It is only necessary to read Galileo's biography to realize how disastrous in 1632 might have been the consequences of an announcement in scientific discovery.

A work entitled "Voyage du Jeune Anacharsis" by the Abbé Barthélemy, published in 1788, mentions alphabetic dials, having hands or pointers which were electrically magnetized; these hands on the clock faces being analogous to Strada's description one hundred and seventy years before.

James Bowman Lindsay in 1854 made calculations to demonstrate that stations in England and Scotland could, without wires, signal across the Atlantic to stations in America.

Sir William Crookes, 1892, reading a paper entitled "Some Possibilities of Electricity," said: "Rays of light will not pierce a wall, nor, as we know only too well, a London fog; but electrical vibrations of a yard or more in wave-length will easily pierce such media, which, to them, will be transparent. Here is revealed the bewildering possibility of telegraphy without wires, posts, cables, or any of our present costly appliances." Again he said that Hertzian rays could be received "on a properly constituted instrument, and by concerted signals messages in the Morse code can thus pass from one operator to another."

Tesla (1893) much in the manner outlined by his patents,[1] predicted the transmission through space and without conductors of electrical oscillations.

Professor Lodge testifies that during the year 1894 Dr. Alexander Muirhead clearly foresaw the telegraphic importance of the transmission of Hertzian waves.

Professor Ayrton, an English scientist, predicted, in 1897, that the time would come when the man with the electromagnetic voice in one part of the world would call to and be heard by the man with the electromagnetic ear at any other part of the world; and just as housemates call to one another in the same dwelling would be the long-distance conversation; excepting that in the latter communication only the selected ear might catch the sound.

[1] See page 38.

DISCOVERY.

Connected with electrical science are four great philosophers, Davy, Faraday, Helmholtz, and Hertz, whose discoveries all but span the nineteenth century; and interwoven with the work of those four discoverers are the important achievements of Joseph Henry, Lord Kelvin, Feddersen, Maxwell, Lodge, Edison and Tesla.

Sir Humphry Davy was born in 1778, and consequently commenced his scientific career with the century. Perhaps his greatest gift to electrical progress was his pupil Michael Faraday. The latter, in 1812, happening to be admitted to one of Davy's lectures, became at first his pupil, then his amanuensis and assistant, and finally in 1827 succeeded Sir Humphry as Professor of Chemistry at the Royal Institution of London. This happy combination in England whereby a great teacher was enabled to bequeath to a disciple equally talented the results of his researches was subsequently duplicated in Germany when Heinrich Hertz became assistant to Helmholtz. It was fortunate also that the early labors of Helmholtz were so timed that he could avail himself of the work already done by Davy and Faraday. The death of Helmholtz at an advanced age in 1894, and of Hertz in the same year as his gifted master, terminated the work of that remarkable quartet of scientists.

Chronologically the thread of discovery begins with Huyghens, a Dutch philosopher (born 1629, died 1693), who was apparently the originator of the undulatory theory which assumes that light is propagated by the vibrations of an imponderable medium called ether; and although for many years after Huyghens the favored idea remained that enunciated by Sir Isaac Newton — that light consists of material particles projected from luminous bodies — Newton's hypothesis has since been rejected,[1] and that of wave-motion is universally recognized.

In 1807, when Sir Humphry Davy decomposed potash by electric-battery power there was inaugurated that wonderfully rapid development in electrical matters which characterized the nineteenth century. To this development Davy gave the initial impulse His was a genius so versatile that Coleridge said, "If Sir Humphry had not been the first chemist of his age, he probably would have been its first poet." At the age of twenty-three Sir Humphry's scientific knowledge and his eloquence were attracting in London brilliant audiences. He delivered a series of lectures on "Agricultural Chemistry," which made an epoch in that science; he discovered the exhilarating effect produced by the breathing of nitrous oxide gas; his lecture on "Some Chemical Agencies of Electricity" obtained for him the prize of the French Institute; and the invention of the miner's safety lamp brought a baronetcy and world-wide fame. Six years subsequent to his electrical decomposition of potash, Davy used the galvanic battery of the Royal Institution, consisting of two thousand pairs of zinc and copper plates, and produced between two carbon electrodes a sparking dis-

---

[1] The Newton hypothesis, sometimes called the "corpuscular theory of light," was successfully controverted by Dr. Thomas Young in 1773, who re-established "the undulatory theory."

charge four inches long in the air, and seven inches long in a vacuum. This constituted the first voltaic arc.

Faraday in 1831 discovered the existence of a current in a hollow coil of wire whenever a permanent magnet or an electromagnet was introduced into, or withdrawn from, its interior. He discovered also the principles of inductive influences between electric currents, and found that different insulating media had varying capacities to produce inductive effects. Maxwell quotes Faraday as saying, " It was allowable to admit that the propagation of electricity might be effected by means of the ether, because it was probable that if this ether existed it could fill another office besides serving as a medium for the transmission of light."

In 1842 Professor Joseph Henry of Princeton, United States, drew attention to the fact that the phenomena accompanying the discharge of a Leyden jar was oscillatory in character, and Helmholtz in 1847 confirmed this. Lord Kelvin in 1853 demonstrated mathematically the oscillatory effect, and Feddersen in 1859 proved it by experiment.

Hermann Helmholtz was born at Potsdam, Prussia, in 1821, and was consequently beginning his life-work when Faraday had reached middle age. Like Davy, Helmholtz was a genius of great versatility. He was first a surgeon in the army, and during his medical practice invented the ophthalmascope, still an indispensable piece of apparatus for the oculist. He was metaphysician, mathematician, physiologist, and physicist. The most famous writing of Helmholtz was his essay on " Conservation of Energy," which firmly established that law ; for by reason of diversified knowledge he was able to bring to its demonstration facts from all departments of science. In the same paper

Helmholtz proclaimed the oscillatory nature of a discharge from the Leyden jar; and explained that the oscillations would grow weaker and weaker until their entire energy was damped out by opposing resistances. By analyzing complex tones Helmholtz made science explain music, and his investigations in the laws of sound did much toward the establishment of modern wave theories. His paper on the vortex motion in fluids was probably the basis for Lord Kelvin's hypothesis that all matter is made up of small vortices of fluid, each rotating about a hollow space. It also helped to formulate Maxwell's proposition.

During the period from 1863 to 1873 there was developed the philosophical demonstration by James Clerk Maxwell, that the propagating medium of electromagnetic waves was identical with that of light; and although he was not able to prove it by experiment, Maxwell was the first who fully understood what is now admitted to be the true nature of electrical phenomena. Thus by 1873 it had been established that light with a velocity of 186,000 miles per second consisted of a wave motion produced in a medium called "ether," which Maxwell defined as "a material substance of a more subtle kind than visible bodies, and supposed to exist in those parts of space which are apparently empty."

Recapitulating, Huyghens in the seventeenth century had proclaimed the existence of ether and the undulatory motion of light, and this was confirmed by Dr. Thomas Young in the eighteenth. In the nineteenth century, Henry, Helmholtz, Kelvin, and Feddersen demonstrated that the discharge of a Leyden jar was oscillatory. Maxwell contended that if the velocity of propagation of electromagnetic disturbance was the same as that of light, which had,

he thought, been proved, then the media through which
either light or electricity was transmitted occupied the
same space and must be identical ; and the difference between their resultant manifestations depended only upon
the lengths of their respective waves. Thus the matter
stood at the death of Maxwell in 1879.

As has been said, Heinrich Hertz was a pupil of Helmholtz. From 1883 to 1885 Hertz occupied at Kiel, Germany, the chair of theoretical physics, and in the latter year
was appointed Professor of Physics in the Technical High
School at Carlsruhe. During the delivery of a lecture at
this institution, and while experimenting with a Leyden jar
and two flat coils of wire, Hertz observed that the discharge
of the jar through one of the coils would induce appreciable
current in the other coil (although the jar was a very small
one), provided *that there was a spark gap in the inducing
coil.* This accidental discovery came to a man who has
since proved to be perhaps the most brilliant experiment-
alist and the ablest physicist the world has seen. Hertz
demonstrated that the reasoning of Maxwell was correct ;
the experiments proving conclusively that the medium which
is vibrated by light and the medium which is vibrated by
electromagnetism is one and the same ; that each travels
with the same velocity ; that waves of electromagnetic
disturbance (now called " Hertzian " waves) are reflected
from conducting surfaces and refracted by dielectric substances ; and are plainly analogous to the reflection of light
from polished surfaces and its refraction through glass
prisms.

" This great discovery of Hertz," says Professor Lodge,
" was by no means his only one. In addition to his well-
known essays on electric waves, which marked an epoch in

experimental physics, no less than eighteen papers, all original, and all important, were, by him, contributed to German periodicals."

After the experiments at Carlsruhe, Hertz in 1889 was called to the chair of physics in the University at Bonn. His health failed, however, and he died at Bonn in 1894. He was the first understandingly to transmit electric waves through ether; and is the most important figure in the history of Wireless Telegraphy. From his discovery in 1886, that etheric vibrations would result from the passing of sparks across an air-gap, began the development of electric transmission without conductors.

From a photograph, by courtesy of the Century Company.

Fig. 2.—Signal Hill, St. John's, Newfoundland. X, Room in which the Message from Cornwall was received.

ACHIEVEMENT.

THE record of operative electric telegraphs begins in 1774 with that of Lesarge at Geneva, Switzerland, and prior to 1837 twelve had been constructed.

In July, 1837, Steinheil operated in England a telegraph line twelve miles long, which, besides its two terminal points, was provided with three intermediate, or way, stations. He used but one wire, employing the earth as a return circuit. There were alarm-bells for "calling," and the signals could be read either by sound, or by ink-marks recorded upon paper.

In 1838 Professor Joseph Henry, of Princeton, making with an electrical machine and Leyden jar a one-inch spark in the top room of his residence, set up induced currents in the cellar of the same building.

During that year Steinheil endeavored, although without success, to utilize the two rails of a steam tramway as a telegraph circuit, but suggested the possibility of doing away altogether with conducting wires.

Professor Morse, who had conceived his idea of the telegraph in 1832, did not succeed in operating it until 1838. His plan was the most practical of any brought forward, and proved the most successful; but he was by no means, as is popularly supposed, the originator of the electric telegraph with wires. There seems, however, to be no doubt but that he was the very first to signal without wires; for on December 16th, 1842, he sent a wireless telegram across a canal eighty feet wide; and in November, 1844, Mr. L. D. Gale, acting under instructions from Professor Morse, made wireless signals across the Susquehanna River at Havre de Grâce, a distance of nearly one mile. In the latter experiment Mr. Gale used, as a source of energy, six pairs of plates in the form of a galvanic battery. He found that the best results were obtained when on each side of the river two plates were immersed near its bank, and were connected by an insulated wire stretched along each shore for a distance three times as great as that which measured either path of the crossing signals.

The few chroniclers of wireless telegraphy have all spoken with respect and affection of Mr. James Bowman Lindsay. Several years after Mr. Gale's experiments on the Susquehanna River, Lindsay, having no knowledge of what Morse had done in America, reached the same results in Scotland. It is said that by gradually increasing his distances, Lindsay succeeded at last in signaling across the Tay where the river is two miles wide. In 1854 Lindsay took out an English patent, of which the following brief is from the Abridgements by the British Commissioners of Patents:

"This invention consists of a method of completing the circuit of electric telegraphs through water without submarine cables or submerged wires extending across such water, water being the connecting and conducting medium for the electric fluid.

"The two wires respectively connected with the battery and signal instrument on one side of the water are attached to metal balls, tubes, or plates placed in the water or in moist ground adjacent to the water. The same arrangement is placed on the other side of the water; and the forward as well as the return current passes between the respective plates.

"It is preferred to place the plates on one side of the water at a greater distance apart than the distance across the water ; but in case this is not practicable, the battery power must be augmented, and the size of the immersed plates increased. It is also necessary to place the plates for the forward current opposite to each other and the plates for the return current opposite to each other."

Though a man of learning, Lindsay had little worldly wisdom. He was one of the best linguists, and for many years employed himself upon a dictionary of fifty languages in one book. He foresaw and accurately predicted the universal employment of electric light and electric power. He thought that by his own plan of wireless telegraphy it would be possible to span the Atlantic Ocean. Lindsay was born in 1799, and died in 1862, residing chiefly at Dundee, Scotland. He was a bachelor, and his life was one of consistent and continuous self-sacrifice to science. It is said that during the year 1835 he lived in one room, which was illumined, however, by an electric lamp whose installation was the work of his own hands. In 1859 he read a paper before the British Association on the subject of "Telegraphing without Wires," and among his hearers were Faraday and Sir William Thompson, now Lord Kelvin. While Lindsay was not an original discoverer in wireless telegraphy, he was a notable pioneer; and his unselfish devotion to learning has won for him deserved distinction.

The invention of the telephone in 1876 and 1877 furnished a detector of great delicacy, and immediately after its discovery novel electrical phenomena were noted. The author in 1877 was an observer of those remarkable inductive effects upon neighboring circuits during the progress of experiments made with Edison's "Singing Telephone" over a wire extending from New York to Saratoga Springs.

During that trial I had a Bell telephone receiver in circuit upon a telegraph wire in my residence on the east side of the Hudson River at Albany. The wire to which the Bell telephone was connected ran parallel in Albany with the transmitting line for possibly three hundred feet; but at no point were the respective circuits less than thirty feet apart. That particular Edison apparatus transmitted simply tones, no words. The receiving record of the Singing Telephone was a series of peculiarly harsh and scraping sounds, so that from the notes of a good soprano singer at the transmitter there were audible at the singing receiver nothing but the different pitches of those tones, all the refinements of sound being lost. Upon the unattached circuits and with a Bell telephone receiver, however, the harsh features were eliminated; and while no articulate word could be distinguished, the musical flow was accurate, smooth, and pleasing. Inductive effects from the same Singing Telephone were also manifest at Providence, R.I., probably by reason of the proximity in New York City of the wires leading to Providence, and those connected with Saratoga.

In 1882 Mr. William H. Preece, Engineer-in-Chief of Government Telegraphs in England, succeeded in signaling across the Solent from England to the Isle of Wight. At two different points plates immersed in the sea near one shore were put in line with similar plates near the opposite shore; and upon each side two of the plates were electrically connected by an over-land conductor. The arrangements of the circuits was the same as that used by Morse in 1842, and by Lindsay in 1854; but for apparatus Mr. Preece had an advantage over his predecessors in that he could use a receiving telephone to detect signals; and he also improved upon former practice by employing as a transmitter, and in place of a contact key, a rapidly vibrating reed called a "buzzer," signals appearing at the receiving end as long and short buzzing sounds. At other times and localities in England Mr. Preece made transmissions in a similar way.

The year 1882 was also that during which Professor Dolbear in America filed his application for United States Letters Patent[1] to protect devices for wireless signaling. His patent is further discussed under "Inventors and Inventions." The distances over which he succeeded in sending impulses are variously reported to have been from half a mile to thirteen miles.

Mr. Edison (1885), using just such inductive effects as were observed in 1877, when his Singing Telephone was tried, signaled through space to a moving train from a wire beside the railway.

The crowning achievement was that of Hertz in 1886. Across the little gap in a ring of wire suspended in a room (there being no electrical contact with the charging apparatus) Hertz made tiny sparks appear, as the result of the passage across another and longer spark gap of the oscillatory discharge from a Leyden jar.

Calzecchi Onesti about 1886 observed the coherency among metal filings produced by the impulsive discharge of a previously electrified wire or coil.

Second in importance only to Hertz is the connection with Wireless Telegraphy of Dr. Oliver Joseph Lodge. This eminent scientist, born in England in 1851, became Professor of Physics at the new University of Liverpool in 1880, and during 1887 was elected a Fellow of the Royal

[1] Printed in full in the Appendix. See also Edison Patent of 1885, p. 96.

Society. At the date of Hertz's first etheric transmission, his English contemporary was conducting experiments along the same lines, and Hertz said that in time Lodge would undoubtedly have reached the same results as himself. Between the filings tube of Onesti, 1886, and that of Branly, 1891, there intervenes an experiment of Dr. Lodge in 1889, described by him to the Institution of Electrical Engineers of London in 1890. He had observed "that two knobs sufficiently close together, far too close to stand any voltage such as an electroscope can show, would, when a spark passes between them, actually cohere, conducting, if a single voltaic cell was in circuit, an ordinary bell-ringing current." With permission there is here presented from Dr. Lodge's "Signalling through Space without Wires," the diagram shown as Fig. 3, and the following description :

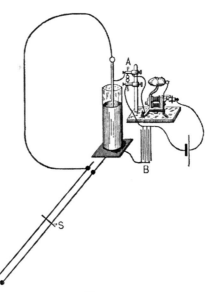

Fig. 3.

"The experiment of the syntonic Leyden jars can be conveniently shown with the double knob or 1889 coherer. The pair of knobs are arranged to connect the coatings of the receiving jar (a large condenser being interposed to prevent their completing a purely metallic circuit), and in circuit with them is a battery and bell. Every time the receiving jar responds syntonically to the electric vibration of the other jar, the knobs cohere (if properly adjusted) and the bell rings. If the bell is free in air it continues ringing until the knobs are gently tapped asunder; but if the bell stands on the same table as the knobs, especially if it rests one foot on the actual stand, then its first stroke taps them back instantly and automatically, and so every discharge of the sending jar is signaled by a single stroke of the bell. Here we have in essence a system of very distinctly syntonic telegraphy, for the jars and their circuits must be accurately tuned together if there is to be any response. A very little error in tuning, easily made by altering the position of the slider (see s, Fig. 3), will make them quite unresponsive unless the distance between them is reduced."

Much of the history of wireless telegraphy after 1889 is set forth in detail in succeeding divisions of this work. Briefly, Branly (1890–1891) made the filings coherer that is sensitive to Hertzian waves. Dr. Lodge in 1893, having learned of Branly's results, commenced a series of experiments, one of which led to inclosing the filings in a vacuum, and another to the making of a more positive de-coherer than was obtained by merely mounting the electric bell upon the base of the filings tube. In 1894 Lodge delivered his famous lecture reviewing the work already done with Hertz's oscillators, with Branly's coherer, and by himself. In 1895 was accomplished the undertaking of Count Popoff of Russia, described under "Inventors and Inventions." In the same year Captain Jackson, by direction of the British Board of Admiralty, passed electrical signals between ships. In 1896 Marconi came to England, and signaled across a space of one hundred yards at the British Post Office in London. Soon afterwards he made a successful trial of two miles overland on Salisbury Plain. In May, 1897, a distance of nine miles over water was attained by Marconi, and from that time his signaling distances were gradually increased until he spanned the ocean.[1]

Guglielmo Marconi was born at Bologna, Italy, on April 25th, 1874. His father is an Italian nobleman, and his mother of Irish nationality. He studied at Leghorn under Professor Rosa, and afterward under Righi at the University of Bologna, of which institution he is a graduate, and has been interested in wireless telegraphy since his sixteenth year. He is of middle height, slim in figure, with blue eyes and brown hair, and his bearing indicates rather a nervous temperament. Upon November 25th, 1901, Mr. Marconi sailed from England, his destination being an experimental station which had been established at Cape Race, some eighty miles from St. Johns, Newfoundland. When interviewed as to this journey by reporters, he said to them that there was a possibility of signaling over three hundred miles of sea, and felt quite sure that two hundred miles would be reached. During that same November, however, the author was privately assured by an official of the Marconi Company in New York City, that within thirty days there would be a record of transatlantic signaling. This prediction was confirmed by the event.

There had been constructed at Poldhu, England, and at Cape Cod, Massachusetts, stations with powerful machinery

[1] " Its progress has not been slow. Five years ago my system worked satisfactorily over a distance of about two miles. Since then its range has been rapidly increased, until, a few months ago, by means of improved and attuned apparatus, a distance of over two hundred miles was successfully bridged, and wireless communication at this distance is now an everyday occurence. A certain commercial application of my system has already been achieved. In all, seventy ships carry permanent installations, and there are over twenty land stations in Great Britain and on the continent of Europe, besides several in this country. To what further extent the system may be commercially applied is not easy to foretell. My recent successful experiments between Poldhu and St. Johns, however, give great hopes of a regular transatlantic wireless telegraph service in the not too distant future."
From Marconi's prefatory note in Century of March, 1902.

for generating electricity; and especial attention had been paid to the vertical conductors or wave-gates by which the ether waves were emitted and received. These structures consisted at either station of twenty poles, each two hundred and ten feet high, by which a large number of wires were supported. The poles and wires, both in America and England, had been damaged by storm, in the latter country the structure at Poldhu being practically destroyed. Neither had been fully replaced. The aerial distance between Poldhu and Cape Cod was some six hundred miles farther than that between Poldhu and Cape Race. Before leaving England, Marconi had arranged with his Engineer at Poldhu to send signals in a certain manner after a date which would be fixed by cablegram, and upon December 9th Poldhu station was instructed (by cable) to begin sending signals every day at three o'clock in the afternoon, and to continue until six o'clock evening, these hours by Newfoundland time being respectively 11.30 A.M. and 2.30 P.M. The signals agreed upon were repetitions of the letter S (by telegraphic code three short marks - - -), to be repeated a certain number of times and then discontinued, for intervals of three minutes' duration.

On Thursday, December 12th, 1901, at 12.30 P.M. Marconi and an assistant, Mr. Kemp, received the first transatlantic signals. During the appointed hours these signals were detected a number of times, and upon the following day, Friday, were again noticed. The public announcement of this event caused great excitement. Marconi was the recipient of congratulatory messages from all over the world, and during the next few weeks he was met everywhere with a series of ovations, the most notable, perhaps, being the dinner held in his honor at the

Waldorf-Astoria Hotel in New York City by the American Institute of Electrical Engineers.

On the first day of March, 1902, Marconi arrived in New York City from England; and declared that he had received on a moving vessel at a position fifteen hundred and fifty-one miles from the sending point [1] an actual message in words; also that he had witnesses to prove beyond peradventure that he had done this through space without wires or cables. Further, that at a distance two thousand and ninety-nine miles [1] from the sending point he had received signals more or less distinct but unmistakable.

The vessel conveying Marconi and his telegraphic devices was the steamship *Philadelphia*. Upon the following day, March 2d, arrived at New York the *Umbria* of the Cunard line; and although the latter ship all the way across the Atlantic had been in the same receiving zone as the *Philadelphia*, and was actually nearer the Cornish coast during the time the latter was receiving messages from England, not a word or signal of those messages was impressed upon the apparatus of the Cunard steamer; although with the *Campania* and *Etruria*, whose instruments were attuned with those upon the *Umbria*, perfect communication was had. The inventor contended that two sets of instruments of different electrical tone might work, without interference, within five inches of each other; that he had two hundred and fifty tunes which would prevent "tapping the circuit"; that the secrecy of the message was complete.[2]

---

[1] See frontispiece.

[2] " It seems to be a matter of popular belief that any receiver within effective range of the transmitter is capable of picking up the messages sent, or, in other words, that there can be no secrecy of communication by my system. Were this so, a very important limitation would be imposed upon the practical usefulness of the system; but by the introduction of important and radical modifications in the original system, and by a systematic application

In the communication between Cornwall and the steamship all the messages were one way, all from the station to the vessel. Mr. Marconi explained that while the *Philadelphia's* equipment admitted the reception of signals, it had not a sufficiently powerful transmitting apparatus to reach to England; but that the Cornwall station could put forth enough energy to overcome that distance.

So far as is generally known, there was from the time of the messages to *S. S. Philadelphia* in March, 1902, no further signaling across the Atlantic until October 31st of the same year, when transoceanic messages were received upon the Italian warship *Carlo Alberto* while that vessel lay at anchor in the harbor of Sydney, Nova Scotia. The wireless telegrams were transmitted from Poldhu. The distance covered is estimated at twenty-three hundred miles. The *Carlo Alberto* had been placed by the King of Italy at Marconi's disposal as an assistance to wireless experiments.

It was on Sunday, December 21st, 1902, one year and nine days after the letter S from Poldhu was heard at Cape Race, that Marconi announced the transmission of three entire messages from Table Head station at Glace Bay, Cape Breton, to Poldhu station in Cornwall, England, viz.: one from the Governor General of Canada to King Edward of England; another from the Commander of the *Carlo Alberto* to the King of Italy; a third to the *Times*, in London, from its special correspondent. The latter was in the nature of formal evidence, and read as follows: —

"Being present at its transmission in Signor Marconi's Canadian station, I have the honor to send the *Times* the inventor's first wireless transatlantic message of greeting to England and Italy."

of the principles of electrical resonance, this objection has, in very great measure, been overcome." — *From Marconi's prefatory note in Century of March, 1902.*

Upon January 19th, 1903, the Marconi Station at Wellfleet, Cape Cod, Massachusetts, transmitted the following :

HIS MAJESTY, EDWARD VII.,
LONDON, ENGLAND.

In taking advantage of the wonderful triumph of scientific research and ingenuity which has been achieved in perfecting a system of wireless telegraphy, I extend on behalf of the American people most cordial greetings and good wishes to you and to all the people of the British Empire.

THEODORE ROOSEVELT.

WELLFLEET, MASS., JAN. 19, 1903.

The reply which follows was returned by cable :

SANDRINGHAM, JAN. 19, 1903.

THE PRESIDENT,
WHITE HOUSE, WASHINGTON, AMERICA.

I thank you most sincerely for the kind message which I have just received from you, through Marconi's transatlantic wireless telegraphy. I sincerely reciprocate in the name of the people of the British Empire the cordial greetings and friendly sentiment expressed by you on behalf of the American Nation, and I heartily wish you and your country every possible prosperity.   EDWARD R. AND I.

Mr. Marconi explained that his apparatus not being quite ready for long-distance operation, the message from President Roosevelt was directed to be relayed by Table Head, Nova Scotia, station. It was found, however, that the Poldhu station in England had been able to copy the telegram while it was being sent to Table Head.

Upon January 21st, 1903, the Italian Government asked for an appropriation of $150,000 to erect, under the direction of Marconi, wireless telegraph stations with a capacity of six thousand miles, for service between Italy and South America.

Fig. 4. — Outside the Cabot Tower on Signal Hill, St. Johns, Newfoundland.

1. Mr. Kemp.   2. Mr. Marconi.   3. Mr. Paget.   4. The keeper of the station.

From a photograph. Copyright by James Vey. By Courtesy of the Century Company.

REESE LIBRARY
OF THE
UNIVERSITY

EXPLANATORY.

WHAT were the devices and methods employed to accomplish the transmissions ?   How were they used ?   Why did they produce the results desired ?

Coherer. — The prime factor is the coherer, which in Fig. 5 to show clearly the position of the grains *g*, that constitute the kernel of the whole matter, is drawn somewhat out of proportion.   Those metallic grains are inclosed in a glass tube, G G G G, between two silver plugs, P and P′; to which plugs are connected platinum wires, W and W′.   When proper action is taken at a transmitting station

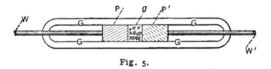

Fig. 5.

the grains *g* at a receiving point *cohere*.   If, after cohesion is established, the glass tube be gently tapped, the grains will separate, i.e., will *decohere*.   When these minute particles are together they close an electric circuit, producing an effect which, on account of the delicacy of the instrument, is rather weak, but which may be made through a relay to close another electric circuit sufficiently powerful to produce either an audible signal, as when a telephone or sounder is used, or to exhibit a visual one, as when ink marks are made upon paper tape. It is also possible, by means of this second and stronger electric circuit, automatically to set in motion, immediately after the mark has been made, a vibrating hammer such as is used in electric door-bells, and which the English call a "trembler." By directing the vibrating hammer against the coherer, or against anything to which the coherer is secured, the grains g may be separated, and the electric devices will then be in position to make another mark.[1]

Signals. — In telegraphy marks, or "signals," are made of two decidedly differing lengths, designated "the long and the short." Combinations of long and short marks are used for letters. Upon the paper ribbon of the wireless telegraph recorder the name of the genius who signaled from Poldhu to Cape Race would appear thus :

M	A	R	C	O	N	I

Circuits. — Fig. 6 is a diagram devoid of many details which will be supplied hereafter in other drawings. Upon the receiving side letters H, B', and R represent respectively a coherer and the battery and relay of the weak electric circuit before noted. On the transmitting side B is a battery, and K a key for closing the primary circuit of a sparking appliance of which P is the primary winding and L the secondary part of a "step-up" induction coil. S G stands for the spark-gap. Upon each closure of the key K, there is produced sufficient strain to cause sparks to fly between terminating electrodes T T of the secondary coil

---

[1] See Fig. 3, Part I., p. 16, and Fig. 31, Part II., p. 98, and accompanying descriptions.

REESE LIBRARY
OF THE
UNIVERSITY
OF
CA...

L.   A A′ are vertical wires which in the first transatlantic transmission were respectively maintained in position by masts at Cornwall and by a kite in Newfoundland.   They are sometimes called "antennae."   It will be seen that at "Transmitter" one of the electrodes T is in connection with the high wire A, while the other is put to earth at E.

When key K is brought onto the anvil V, an electric circuit is made, and the current in it by inductive influence is

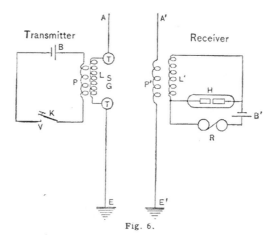

Fig. 6.

communicated to the secondary coil and raised in pressure. The sparking across S G becomes the center of a disturbance from which waves spread in all directions.   These are picked up by any vertical wire as A′ and pass through P′ to earth at E′.   In the receiving apparatus, the sparking (exceedingly weak by reason of dissipation of the energy on the long journey), being "stepped up" from P′ to L′ is now through the filings at H, causing them to cohere, the relay R is energized through coherer, and by a local circuit (not shown in Fig. 6) a mark is made.

In a general way the action just described is what took place at Newfoundland when the Poldhu station sent the letter s, three short marks. It was also the method employed to send from Poldhu to the *S. S. Philadelphia* at sea. In the trial to Newfoundland the receiving station used an ordinary hand (listening) telephone in place of the relay R shown in Fig. 6, a telephone receiver being much more sensitive than a relay. Upon the *Philadelphia*, however, ink-marks were recorded upon paper tape.

TUNING.

It will be remembered that immediately after the Cornwall-Newfoundland demonstration, Marconi, upon being asked if it were not probable that he received the signal s from some ship or station other than the Cornwall plant, replied, "It is impossible; I was tuned only for Poldhu."

Theory of Electrical Resonance. — To understand the devices used for electrical tuning it will be necessary to consider first the theory by which "electrical resonance" is explained, and then the analogies that are used to demonstrate that theory.

It is supposed that all matter, solid, liquid, or gaseous, is made up of molecules; and that these molecules are combinations of atoms of different chemical elements, atoms being quantitatively the smallest divisions of matter, and an element an individual substance, as distinguished from those substances which are a combination of two or more elementary kinds of matter. The density, and to an extent the weight, of any substance depends upon the nearness of the molecules to one another. In air, or other gases, they are widely separated. In metals they are very close to one another. In either substance there is between them space, and that space is said to be permeated by "ether." Scientists have not yet added a fourth dimension to length, breadth, and thickness ; but the three divisions of matter are now supplemented by a fourth, and they speak of the solid, the liquid, the gas, and the ether.

Analogy of Jelly. — An analogy to ether and matter is furnished by the contents of a vessel containing a mixture of lead bullets and jelly. Imagine the jelly to be so tremulous as to be capable of vibrating from a disturbance by which the bullets, being much more inert, move so little as to be practically still. Further imagine that the jelly be made to oscillate, being first pushed forward and then pulled backward, very rapidly. It will readily be understood that before the forward motion of the jelly has overcome the inertia of the bullets, the backward one will have reversed and neutralized that motion.

Analogy of a Pool of Water. — If a person standing upon one side of a pool of water strikes into the water with a paddle each time in the same direction and at regular intervals, so that he maintains a rhythmical beat, it will be found that after each stroke and up to a certain maximum the waves caused by the paddle will augment in size ; but that if strokes be afterward made at irregular intervals the waves will decrease in volume. Discord will tend to undo the work that has been done by rhythm.

Analogy of Spring and Timber. — Suppose, as in Fig. 7, a stick of timber L is suspended from a rigid support E by a spiral steel spring C, and that the timber be given a push upward, or a push downward, then it will vibrate a certain number of times per minute.   If it be pushed gently it will move slowly through a small space, if pushed forcibly it will move more quickly through a greater space ; but the oscillations in a unit of time will always be the same.   This rate of vibration is governed by the resiliency of the spring C and the weight of the load L.   If the resiliency of the spring be increased, or the weight of the timber be decreased, the rate of vibration will be quickened.   If C be made less springy, or L be made heavier, the rate will be slower.

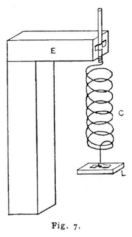

Fig. 7.

slower.   To change the rate by altering either or both of the conditions has been called by clockmakers " regulating " ; Scientists of to-day call it " tuning."

Advantages of Harmonious Action. — The pushing if continued should, in order to get the best results, be in accord with the rate of the apparatus ; that is to say, the strokes must be exactly as many per minute, or exactly one-half as many, or twice as many, or some even division or multiple of the rate.   Irregular strokes will tend to stop the motion just as in the case of the paddle and waves. Now set the timber L upon the surface of the water on one side of a pool of considerable width, and so that the crest of a small wave will just uplift it.   By moving the timber and timing its oscillations the rate may be ascer-

tained. If the water upon the far side of the pool be struck
with the paddle time after time at the timber's rate, waves
will spread from the paddle ; and although only a few faint
ripples may reach the timber-and-spring-device they will
be attuned to it, and, if the strokes be regularly continued,
each wave will tend to increase the length of the oscillation
of the spring.

At Poldhu a powerful source of vibration was sending
waves into the ether, and the little ripples were caught at
Newfoundland by a delicate receiving apparatus which had
been adjusted to vibrate at the same rate as the Cornwall
transmitter.

Fig. 8 represents a guitar, which instrument may be
used to demonstrate the fact that air waves when set in

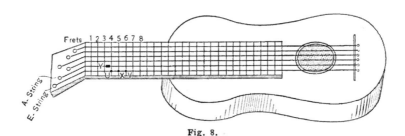

Fig. 8.

motion by one string of a certain note will cause to vibrate
another string tuned to the same note. In trying this
experiment, to avoid troublesome stretching of strings, it
will be advisable to keep about a half-tone below "concert
pitch." When the A string is brought to such tension as
to be in its proper relative tune with the E string, it will
sound in unison with the latter, whenever the E is stopped
by the finger pressing the E firmly against fret 5.

Mechanical Tuning. — To ascertain if the two notes are in unison, cut a piece of medium writing-paper to a size about five-eighths of an inch square, fold it one way in the middle and set it astride of the open A string. When the two strings are properly tuned, and the E string is struck below the stopped point at fret 5, the paper on A will vibrate so strongly as to be perceptible both to the eye and also by a buzzing noise to the ear. If now the E string be stopped either on the 4th or the 6th fret, or if the tension on the A string be increased or decreased in the slightest degree, the paper will remain motionless, no matter how violently the E string may be set in motion. Such an operation is sometimes called "mechanical tuning," and more accurate results may be obtained than by the usual method of listening.

Referring back to the spring and timber demonstration in a pool of water (Fig. 7), the weight of the A string is analogous to that of the timber, the tension upon it to the elasticity of the spring. The stopped E sets up waves of exactly the same rate as those to which A is attuned.

In the pool the waves are of water moving a few feet per second. In the guitar demonstration the waves are of air moving at the rate of 1400 or 1500 feet per second. In the transatlantic transmission of Marconi the waves were of ether, traveling 186,000 miles per second.

Electrical Resonance in Practice. — It is hoped that the foregoing illustrations will make clear the principles of electrical resonance. The practice is illustrated in Fig. 9.

Transmitting Side. — B is a battery or other source of energy. P is the primary winding of an induction coil,

and K the key of transmission. L is a secondary winding complementary to the primary P.   T T are electrodes
of S G the spark-gap. C is a condenser.   P2 and L2 are
respectively the primary and secondary of another induction coil in the transmitting apparatus which may, by way
of distinction, be called a transformer, its function being
to convert the waves that oscillate in the spark-gap to a
still higher intensity.   D is a variable inductive resistance

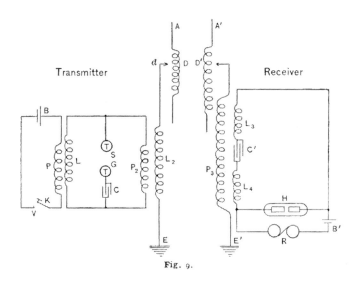

Fig. 9.

placed in the circuit between the vertical wire or wave-gate
A and the earth at E.   At the transmitter the condenser
C is analogous to the resiliency of the stopped E string of
Fig. 8, and L 2 and D represent the inertia of the spring,
or the load. By moving the pointer *d* the load may be
changed, and by giving the condenser more or less surface
the force of oscillation may be intensified or diminished.

Receiving Side. — Looking now at the receiver in Fig. 9 A' is the vertical wire. The changeable inductive resistance D' and primary coil P 3 of a transformer is placed in that part of the wave circuit which reaches from A' to the earth at E'. D' with P3 constitute the load, being analogous to the timber in Fig. 7. Inductive transference of the waves from P3, to L3 and L4, increase the intensity of the faint ripples which come through space from the vertical wire A of transmitter. C' is a condenser placed in a bight of the long wire which forms the secondary winding of L3, L4. This condenser (C') represents the steel spring C of Fig. 7. In tuning the receiver, either the load D' P3, or the spring C' may be changed to increase or decrease the rate of the receiver. Infinitesimal waves passing through the gaps in metallic powder of H will cause those grains to cohere, and so close the electric circuit H B' R. Relay R translates the signal into a more powerful local circuit, which actuates an ink-marking register, and, at the same time, causes a " tapper "[1] (not shown in Fig. 9) to strike the glass tube H and " decohere " the powder. The apparatus is then ready for another signal.

LOCALIZATION.

The following extract of a letter from Dr. A. Fleming, which was published in the *London Times*, October 4, 1900, will serve to define and illustrate the term used as a heading for this division :

Two operators at St. Catherine's, Isle of Wight, were instructed to send simultaneously two different wireless messages to Poole, Dorset, and without delay or mistake the two were correctly recorded and printed down at

[1] Similar to the device shown in Fig. 31, Part II.

the same time in Morse signals on the tapes of the two corresponding receivers at Poole.

In this first demonstration each receiver was connected to its own independent aerial wire, hung from the same mast. But greater wonders followed. Mr. Marconi placed the receivers at Poole one on the top of the other, and connected them both to one and the same wire, about forty feet in length, attached to the mast. I then asked to have two messages sent at the same moment by the operator at St. Catherine's, one in English and the other in French. Without failure, each receiver at Poole rolled out its paper tape, the message in English perfect on one, and that in French on the other. When it is realized that these visible dots and dashes are the result of trains of intermingled electric waves rushing with the speed of light across the intervening thirty miles, caught on one and the same short aerial wire and disentangled and sorted out automatically by the two machines into intelligible messages in different languages, the wonder of it all cannot but strike the mind.

Your space is too valuable to be encroached upon by further details, or else I might mention some marvelous results exhibited by Mr. Marconi during the same demonstrations, of messages received from a transmitter thirty miles away, and recorded by an instrument in a closed room merely by the aid of a zinc cylinder, four feet high, placed on a chair.[1] More surprising is it to learn that, while these experiments have been proceeding between Poole and St. Catherine's, others have been taking place for the admiralty between Portsmouth and Portland, these lines of communication intersecting each other; yet so perfect is the independence that nothing done on one circuit now affects the other, unless desired.

Mr. Marconi has insisted that his transmitted signals are perfectly localized. He has even challenged Professor Lodge and Mr. Preece either to interrupt or to intercept them, offering the use of his company's stations should those eminent scientists desire to experiment. If, however, they try, and fail to catch the signals, it does not follow that human ingenuity will never succeed in doing so. Unless, indeed, Marconi has means other than those generally known to the electrical profession, it is believed that "syntony," as it is called, is a combination not difficult to unlock.

[1] See Fig. 37, Part II.

The company's experts claim first, that their spark-gap will not be known to unauthorized persons; again, that their coherer may be made so insensitive that it will answer only to a considerable force at the sending station, and that all energies less than theirs will not affect it; again, that in addition to a knowledge of the force required it will be necessary for the intercepter to know the self-induction (the load) and the condenser effect (the resiliency). It would seem, however, that it is not necessary to ascertain *each* of these facts, but merely to find the *rate of beat* to which the coherer will respond, and that may be any combination of load and spring which will produce the right wave-motion. If, then, a would-be tapper-in exposes a number of coherers differently sensitized, and with each coherer connected with a maximum or a minimum condenser effect, he will need only to vary the load upon each coherer, which may be very rapidly done. Having found the "rate," he may "interrupt" as well as "intercept."

QUANTITATIVE DATA.

Power. — In quantitative terms authorized statements in the March *Century*, 1902, give the energy used in the Cornwall-Newfoundland transmission as being supplied by a 40 h. p. alternating current dynamo, having an initial pressure of two thousand volts which was "stepped up" to fifty thousand volts. There were at Poldhu twenty[1] masts, each two hundred and ten feet high, the conductors upon each mast being in electrical connection with all the others. The metal spheres forming high-tension terminals

[1] See Fig. 66, Part IV.

of the transformers were separated by a distance which
varied from about $\frac{4}{10}$ inch to about $\frac{8}{10}$ inch. At the
Newfoundland station the aerial wire was elevated by a
kite to an altitude of about four hundred feet ; its swaying
varied the altitude, which variation was a serious obstacle
to the uniform reception of signals. The coherer used
was a small glass tube one and one-half inches long and
one-tenth inch internal diameter. Within the tube were
tightly fitted two silver plugs separated $\frac{1}{30}$ inch. This little space was partly filled with a mixture of nickel and silver filings to which a trace of mercury had been added.[1]

**Comparative Speed of Signal Propagation by Wireless
Telegraph and by Cables.** — Marconi has said to his English stockholders that whereas the speed of the submarine
cable is directly affected by length of transmission, the
wireless system is not in the least affected by distance.
That "it is just as easy to work at high speed across the
Atlantic or Pacific as to work across the English Channel."
He is confident of establishing direct communication between England and New Zealand.[2]   He says that the curvature of the earth does not affect the signals, and that
ultimately he will be able to send them all around the
world.

Marconi's Conclusions. — From that excellent article in
the *Century Magazine* of March, 1902, already mentioned,
there is a summing up of Marconi's conclusions at that
date.

Wireless telegraphy is most effective over marine areas.
Over low lying country two-thirds of marine distance may

[1] See description of " silver coherer " in Part IV.
[2] See chart, Fig. 39.

be reached, but over ordinary diversified country the po-
tency of vibrations is reduced to one-half what it is at sea.
High hills do not constitute an obstacle, but the ground
itself retards the signals.   The vibrations seem to reach
slightly farther in fog than in fine weather.   Atmospheric
conditions do not seriously affect the signals.   Electrical
disturbances are their only foe.   Indications are that a
pole two hundred feet high gives the best results.   With a
a balloon or kite elevated to four hundred feet, the wire
must necessarily be very slight, and the ceaseless swaying
of the upholder also interferes.   A horizontal wire (as an
antenna) gives no energy.   No advantage in marine signaling is gained by setting a pole on a high hill.   Proximity
to the sea is desirable and a low-lying spit of land the best.
Some geological formations are perverse, others are responsive.

DESCRIPTIVE.

TESLA [1] IN WIRELESS TRANSMISSION.

Tesla's Proposed Plan of 1893. —— Nikola Tesla devoted himself early to the problem of transmitting electrical energy without wires, not only for telegraphic, but also for industrial purposes. In February and March, 1893, he delivered lectures before the Franklin Institute in Philadelphia and the National Electric Light Association in St. Louis, in which he advanced a plan of wireless transmission, and expressed his conviction that " it certainly is possible to produce some electrical disturbance sufficiently powerful to be perceptible by suitable instruments at any point of the earth's surface."

In describing his plan in detail he says :

" Assume that a source of alternating currents, s, be connected, as in Fig. 10, with one of its terminals to earth (convenient to the water mains), and

Fig. 10.

with the other to a body of large surface, P. When the electric oscillation is set up, there will be a movement of electricity in and out of P, and

1 TESLA, NIKOLA, born at Smiljan, Lika. Austria-Hungary, in 1857. A noted physicist and electrician. He came to the United States in 1884 with a view of developing motors based on his discovery of the rotating magnetic field ; this he completed in 1888. He has invented a number of methods and appliances in the line of electrical vibrations aiming at the production of efficient light with lamps without filaments, and the production and transmission of power and intelligence without wires. On his discovery of the action of air or gaseous matter when subjected to rapidly alternating electrostatic stresses is based the modern art of insulating currents of very high tension. He has also constructed steam-engines and electrical generators (oscillators) with which otherwise unattainable results are obtained. — Century Dictionary and Cyclopedia, 1895.

alternating currents will pass through the earth, converging to or diverging from the point C, where the ground connection is made. In this manner neighboring points on the earth's surface within a certain radius will be disturbed. But the disturbance will diminish with the distance, and the distance at which the effect will still be perceptible will depend on the quantity of electricity set in motion. Since the body P is insulated, in order to displace a considerable quantity the potential of the source must be excessive, since there would be limitations as to the surface of P. The conditions might be adjusted so that the generator, or source, s, will set up the same electrical movement as though its circuit were closed. Thus it is certainly practicable by means of proper machinery to impress an electric vibration, at least of a certain low period, upon the earth. Theoretically it should not require a great amount of energy to produce a disturbance perceptible at great distance, or even all over the surface of the globe. Now, it is quite certain that at any point within a certain radius of the source, s, a properly adjusted self-induction and capacity device can be set in action by resonance. Not only can this be done, but another source, s,[1] Fig. 10, similar to s or any number of such sources, may be set to work in synchronism with the latter, and the vibration thus intensified and spread over a large area; or a flow of electricity produced to or from the source s,[1] if the same be of opposite phase to the source, s. Proper apparatus must first be produced, by means of which the problem can be attacked, and I have devoted much thought to this subject."

In the same lectures he showed a number of novel experiments, among which was the operation of a variety of devices by using one wire, instead of two as is usual in electrical connections. He continued investigations along these lines, and in 1898 had already developed apparatus of great power, giving a pressure of four million volts and discharges extending through sixteen feet, which at that time were considered remarkable.[1]

Tesla's First Two Patents on Methods and Apparatus for the Wireless Transmission of Energy. — The patents are numbered 645,576 and 649,621, and were issued

[1] See Electrical Review, New York, October 26, 1898.

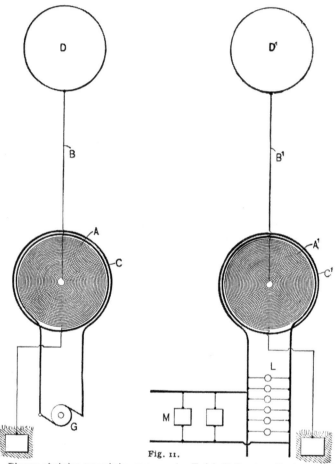

Fig. 11.

Diagram of wireless transmission accompanying Tesla's U. S. patents No. 645,576 and No. 649,621. The transmitter comprises a generator of electric oscillations G, a primary conductor C, and a secondary coil A B, which is connected to ground and to an elevated terminal D, and tuned to the oscillations of the generator. The receiving apparatus has a similarly arranged coil A′ D′ tuned to the transmitted oscillations, and associated with a secondary circuit containing the receiving devices. The terminals D and D′ are maintained above the surrounding objects, the height being determined by the amount and quality of the work to be performed. The length of the grounded conductors A D and A′ D′ is preferably made equal to one quarter of the wave length of the oscillations. The transmitter and receiver may be thousands of miles apart.

respectively March 20th, and May 15th, 1900. The original application covering both inventions was filed September
2nd, 1897. The system, as described by the inventor in
these patents, is radically different from the Hertzian, both
in the methods and apparatus employed. In the Hertzian
system, the energy is transmitted to the receiver by electro-magnetic waves which pass out laterally from the
transmitting wire into space. In Tesla's system the energy
radiated is not used, but a current is led to earth and to
an elevated terminal, and the energy is transmitted by a
process of conduction. Quoting from one of his patents :

"It is to be noted that the phenomenon here involved in the transmission of electrical energy is one of true conduction, and is not to be
confounded with the phenomena of electrical radiation which have heretofore been observed, and which, from the very nature and mode of propagation, would render practically impossible the transmission of any appreciable amount of energy to such distances as are of practical importance."

The arrangement of his transmitting and receiving
circuits is illustrated in Fig. 11, and will be understood
with reference to the explanatory note.

As characteristic of these inventions the following two
claims may be quoted :

" The method hereinbefore described of transmitting electrical energy
through the natural media, which consists in producing at a generating
station a very high electrical pressure, causing thereby a propagation or
flow of electrical energy, by conduction, through the earth and the air
strata, and collecting or receiving at a distant point the electrical energy so
propagated or caused to flow.

The combination with a transmitting coil or conductor connected to
ground and to an elevated terminal respectively, and means for producing
electrical currents or oscillations in the same, of a receiving coil or conductor similarly connected to ground and to an elevated terminal, the said coil
or coils having a length equal to one-quarter of the wave length of the
disturbance propagated, as set forth."

Description of Transmitter Giving Four Million Volts. —
In describing a special apparatus Tesla says :

" The transmitting apparatus was in this case one of my electrical
oscillators, which are transformers of a special type, now well known and
characterized by the passage of oscillatory discharges of a condenser
through the primary.   The source G, forming one of the elements of the
transmitter, was a condenser of a capacity of about four one-hundredths of
a microfarad, and was charged from a generator of alternating currents of
fifty thousand volts pressure, and discharged by means of a mechanically
operated break five thousand times per second through the primary C.
The latter consisted of a single turn of stout, stranded cable of inappreciable
resistance and of an inductance of about eight thousand centimeters, the
diameter of the loop being very nearly two hundred and forty-four centimeters.   The total inductance of the primary circuit was approximately ten
thousand centimeters, so that the primary circuit vibrated generally according to adjustment, from two hundred and thirty thousand to two hundred
and fifty thousand times per second.   The high-tension coil A in the form
of a flat spiral was composed of fifty turns of heavily insulated cable No. 8
wound in one single layer, the turns beginning close to the primary loop
and ending near its center.   The outer end of the secondary or high-tension
coil A was connected to the ground.

The primary and secondary circuits in the transmitting apparatus being
carefully synchronized, an electromotive force from two to four million volts
and more was obtainable at the terminals of the secondary coil A."

Curious Phenomena Produced. — Tesla's apparatus seems
to be capable of peculiar actions.   He says :

" For example, a conductor or terminal, to which impulses such as those
here considered are supplied, but which is otherwise insulated in space and
is remote from any conducting-bodies, is surrounded by a luminous flame-like
brush or discharge often covering many hundreds or even as much as
several thousands of square feet of surface, this striking phenomenon clearly
attesting the high degree of conductivity which the atmosphere attains
under the influence of the immense electrical stresses to which it is
subjected.   This influence is, however, not confined to that portion of the
atmosphere which is discernible by the eye as luminous, and which, as has
been the case in some instances actually observed, may fill the space within
a spherical or cylindrical envelope of a diameter of sixty feet or more, but
reaches out to far remote regions, the insulating qualities of the air being,

NIKOLA TESLA.

as I have ascertained, still sensibly impaired at a distance many hundred times that through which the luminous discharge projects from the terminal and in all probability much farther."

The conductivity imparted to the air by these currents Tesla proposes to utilize in the wireless transmission of power on an industrial scale.

Transmission of Enormous Energy Over Vast Distances. — " From my experiments and observations I conclude *that with electromotive impulses not greatly exceeding fifteen or twenty million volts the energy of many thousands of horse-power may be transmitted over vast distances, measured by many hundreds and even thousands of miles, with terminals not more than thirty to thirty-five thousand feet above the level of the sea ;* and even this *comparatively small elevation* will be required chiefly for reasons of economy, and if desired it may be considerably reduced, since, by such means as have been described, practically any potential that is desired may be obtained and the currents through the air strata may be rendered very small, whereby the loss in the transmission may be reduced. It will be understood that the transmitting as well as the receiving coils, transformers, or other apparatus may be in some cases movable — as, for example, when they are carried by *vessels floating in the air,* or by ships at sea."

To express this idea in other language, if one captive balloon were put at seven miles' elevation over Niagara Falls, and another balloon at the same height in France, energy from a dynamo at the former station might without undue loss in transmission be made to set in motion upon French territory electric motors, or to supply the power to illumine electric lamps.

Tesla's "Telautomata." — On July 1, 1898, Mr. Tesla filed an application for another American Patent, No. 613,809.   Its first claim is an excellent brief.   It reads:

" The improvement in the art of controlling the movements and operation of a vessel or vehicle herein described, which consists in producing waves or disturbances which are conveyed to the vessel by the natural media, actuating thereby suitable apparatus on the vessel and effecting the control of the propelling engine, the steering and other mechanism by the operation of the said mechanism as set forth."

Methods Described. — The inventor describes a number of methods for producing waves.   The preferred one seems to be the "passing through the conducting path currents of a specially designed high frequency alternator, or, better still, those of a strongly charged condenser," and then "adjusting the circuit on the moving body so as to be in exact electromagnetic synchronism with the primary disturbances;" and he says that in such a way "this influence may be utilized at great distances."

Application to Warfare. — In summing up the many useful purposes to which this invention may be applied, the pantentee thinks its "greatest value will result from its effect upon warfare and armaments, for by reason of its certain and unlimited destructiveness it will tend to bring about and maintain perfect peace among nations."   It may be inferred that this refers more especially to the moving and direction of torpedoes.

In the Tesla system methods of electrical conversion by means of condenser discharges and the so-called "Tesla coil" play an important part.   The earliest records of these inventions in the U. S. Patent Office date from 1891.

Method of Electrical Conversion by Condenser Discharges. — This method is described in Patent Number 462,418 of November 3, 1891 (application filed February 4, 1891).

Quoting in the language of the inventor:

"I employ a generator, preferably of very high tension, and capable of yielding either direct or alternating currents. This generator I connect up with a condenser or conductor of some capacity, and discharge the accumulated electrical energy disruptively through an air-space or otherwise into a working circuit containing translating devices and, when required, condensers. These discharges may be of the same direction or alternating and intermittent, succeeding each other more or less rapidly or oscillating to and fro with extreme rapidity. In the working circuit, by reason of the condenser action, the current impulses or discharges of high tension and small volume are converted into currents of lower tension and greater volume. The production and application of a current of such rapid oscillations or alternations (the number may be many millions per second) secures,

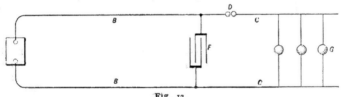

Fig. 12.

among others, the following exceptional advantages: First, the capacity of the condensers for a given output is much diminished; second, the efficiency of the condensers is increased and the tendency to become heated reduced; and, third, the range of conversion is enlarged. I have thus succeeded in producing a system or method of conversion radically different from what has been done heretofore — first, with respect to the number of impulses, alternations, or oscillations of current per unit of time, and, second, with respect to the manner in which the impulses are obtained. To express this result, I define the working current as one of an excessively small period or of an excessively large number of impulses or alternations or oscillations per unit of time, by which I mean not a thousand or even twenty or thirty thousand per second, but many times that number, and one which is made intermittent, alternating, or oscillating of itself without the employment of mechanical devices."

Referring to the diagram in Fig. 12 :

"A represents a generator of high tension; B B, the conductors which lead out from the same. To these conductors are connected the conductors C of a working circuit containing translating devices, such as incandescent lamps or motors G. In one or both conductors B is a break D, the two ends being separated by an air-space or a film of insulation, through which a disruptive discharge takes place. F is a condenser, the plates of which are connected to the generating-circuit.

The discharges will follow each other the more rapidly the more nearly the rate of supply from the generator equals the rate at which the circuit including the generator is capable of taking up and getting rid of the energy. Since the resistance and self-induction of the working circuit C and the rapidity of the successive discharges may be varied at will, the current strengths in the working and in the generating circuit may bear to one another any desired relation.

Tesla Coil.— This invention is first described in Patent No. 454,622 of June 23, 1891 (application filed April 5th, 1891). In the description the inventor says :

"To produce a current of very high frequency and very high potential, certain well-known devices may be employed. For instance, as the primary source of current or electrical energy, a continuous-current generator may be used, the circuit of which may be interrupted with extreme rapidity by mechanical devices, or a magneto-electric machine specially constructed to yield alternating currents of very small period may be used, and in either case, should the potential be too low, an induction-coil may be employed to raise it ; or, finally, in order to overcome the mechanical difficulties, which in such cases become practically insuperable before the best results are reached, the principle of the disruptive discharge may be utilized. By means of this latter plan I produce a much greater rate of change in the current than by the other means suggested, and in illustration of my invention I shall confine the description of the means or apparatus for producing the current to this plan, although I would not be understood as limiting myself to its use. The current of high frequency, therefore, that is necessary to the successful working of my invention, I produce by the disruptive discharge of the accumulated energy of a condenser maintained by charging said condenser from a suitable source and discharging it into or through a circuit under proper relations of self-induction, capacity, resistance, and period in well-understood ways. Such a discharge is known to be, under proper conditions, intermittent or oscillating in character, and in this way a current varying in strength at an enormously rapid rate may be produced. Having produced in the above manner a current of excessive frequency, I obtain from it by means of an induction-coil enormously high potentials — that is to say, in the circuit through which or into which the disruptive discharge of the condenser takes place I include the primary of a suitable induction-coil, and by a secondary coil of much longer and finer wire I convert to currents of extremely high-potential."

With reference to the diagram Fig. 13.

"G is the primary source of current or electrical energy. I have explained above how various forms of generator might be used for this purpose; but in the present illustration I assume that G is an alternating-current generator of comparatively low electromotive force. Under such circumstances I raise the potential of the current by means of an induction-coil having a primary P and a secondary S. Then by the current developed in this secondary I charge a condenser C, and this condenser I discharge through or into a circuit A, having an air-gap a, or, in general, means for maintaining a disruptive discharge. By the means above described a current of enormous frequency is produced. My object is next to convert this into a working-circuit of very high potential, for which purpose I connect up in the circuit A the primary P' of an induction coil having a long fine wire secondary S'. The current in the primary P' develops in the secondary S' a current or electrical effect of corresponding frequency, but of enormous difference of potential."

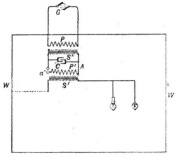

Fig. 13.

Tesla has invented and patented numerous modifications of apparatus embodying these principles. One of the features in his later patents, for which great advantages are claimed, is a series of tuned circuits of high frequency exciting one another.

System of Concatenated Tuned Circuits. — In his patent No. 568,178 of September 22, 1896 (application filed June 20, 1896), the inventor says in setting forth the invention:

"It is well known that every electric circuit, provided its ohmic resistance does not exceed certain definite limits, has a period of vibration of its own analogous to the period of vibration of a weighted spring. In order to alternately charge a given circuit of this character by periodic impulses impressed upon it, and to discharge it most effectively, the frequency of the impressed impulses should bear a definite relation to the frequency of vibration possessed by the circuit itself. Moreover, for like reasons, the period or vibration of the discharge-circuit should bear a similar relation to the impressed impulses or the period of the charging-circuit. When the conditions are such that the general law of harmonic vibrations is followed, the circuits are said to be in resonance or in electromagnetic synchronism, and this condition I have found in my system to be highly advantageous. Hence, in practice, I adjust the electrical constants of the circuits so that in normal operation, this condition of resonance is approximately attained.

Any departure from this condition will result in a decreased output, and this fact I take advantage of in regulating such output by varying the frequencies of the impulses or vibrations in the several circuits.

Inasmuch as the period of any given circuit depends upon the relations of its resistance, self induction, and capacity, a variation of any one or more of these may result in a variation in its period. There are, therefore, various ways in which the frequences of vibration of the several circuits in the system referred to may be varied, but the most practicable and efficient ways of accomplishing the desired result, are the following: (a) varying the rate of the impressed impulses of current, or those which are directed from the source of supply into the charging-circuit, as by varying the speed of the commutator or other circuit-controller; (b) varying the self-induction of the charging-circuit; (c) varying the self-induction or capacity of the discharge circuit.

Intensifying Electric Oscillations by Means of Refrigerant. — Another suggestion from Mr. Tesla is to employ as a means of increasing the intensity of electric oscillations a refrigerant. He says that "when a circuit adapted to vibrate freely is maintained at a low temperature, the

THE TESLA WIRELESS PLANT ON LONG ISLAND.

oscillations excited in the same are to an extraordinary degree magnified and prolonged, and that he is thus enabled to produce many valuable results which have heretofore been wholly impracticable " The cooling agent may be any freezing mixture. Liquid air is instanced. In the transmission of etheric waves, he would apply this refrigerant to coils — both at the transmitting and at the receiving ends. He says that the circuits at either end of the transmission should have the greatest possible self-induction and the smallest possible resistance. The invention is fully described in Patent No. 685,012 of October 22, 1901. (Application filed March 21, 1900.)

Methods of Storing the Energy Transmitted, and Strengthening Feeble Impulses. — In another series of patents, bearing the numbers 685,953, 685,954, 686,955, and 685,956, all granted in 1901, Tesla advances other improvements in the transmission and utilization of electrical energy. The fundamental idea underlying these inventions is to store the energy transmitted in a condenser during any desired time interval, and to utilize the stored energy, either directly to operate a receiving device, or to control another circuit including the same. In a modification of the apparatus the latter circuit charges a condenser, and the impulses transmitted are used to control the charge of the condenser. In order to effect a charging by the impulses conveyed from distance, they are commutated either by a mechanical device or by means of an electric valve with stationary electrodes. In a special arrangement shown, the energy accumulated in the condenser is discharged through the primary of an induction coil, the secondary of which is used for the purpose of controlling the operation of a

delicate receiver.   In this way almost any degree of sensitiveness which may be desired can be attained.   On this
point the inventor says :

> " It will be seen that by the use of my invention results hitherto
> unattainable in utilizing disturbances or effects transmitted through natural
> media may be readily attained, since, however great the distance of such
> transmission, and however feeble or attenuated the impulses received,
> enough energy may be accumulated from them by storing up the
> energy of succeeding impulses for a sufficient interval of time to render
> the sudden liberation of it highly effective in operating a receiver."

Improved Mercury Interrupters. — In order to avoid
waste of energy and deterioration of the electrodes, Tesla
has designed a great variety of mercury interrupters, on
which he has obtained a number of patents dated 1897
and 1898. In these devices the circuit is made and broken
in an hermetically inclosed space and the wear of the electrodes entirely prevented, the contact surfaces being constituted of mercury.   In some forms an inert gas under
great pressure is employed to improve the action, the
inventor claiming that he has discovered that "a gas under
great compression nearly fulfills the ideal requirements."

New Methods of Individualization. — Instead of relying on
simple tuning, Tesla has developed a new principle, which is
set forth in his last two patents bearing the numbers 723,-
188 and 725,605 (original application filed July 16, 1900).
In this invention the transmitter is made to give two, or
a greater number, of different vibrations, simultaneously or
in a certain order of succession.   The receiver again has
a number of tuned circuits, each of which responds to
one of the vibrations of the transmitter, and the arrangement is such that only when all the receiving circuits are

affected the indicating instrument is made to operate. By the use of this principle "a degree of safety against mutual and extraneous interference is attained, such as is comparable to that of a combination lock." On the other hand, any desired number of instruments can be simultaneously operated through the earth or other conducting channel. The improvement is not limited to wireless telegraphy. "It will be seen," says the inventor, "from a consideration of the nature of the method, that the invention is applicable not only in the special manner described, in which the transmission of the impulses is effected through the natural media, but for the transmission of energy for any purpose and whatever the medium through which the impulses are conveyed."

Marvelous Effects Produced by Oscillators of Great Power. — Early in 1889 Tesla went to Colorado to develop his methods and apparatus for the transmission of wireless energy, and to ascertain the laws of propagation of electrical waves through the earth. Upon his return he published an article which appeared in the "Century" of June, 1900, in which photographic views of some experiments with one of his oscillators were shown. It appears that with these machines there is no limit to the intensity of the effects and magnitude of the forces produced. According to Tesla even interplanetary space may be bridged by the terrific commotions of such an oscillator. He says:

"However extraordinary the results shown may appear, they are but trifling compared with those which are attainable by apparatus designed on these same principles. I have produced electrical discharges, the actual path of which, from end to end, was probably more than one hundred feet long; but it would not be difficult to reach lengths one hundred times as great. I have produced electrical movements occurring at the rate of approximately one hundred thousand horse-power, but rates of one, five, or ten million horse-power are easily practicable. In these experiments effects were developed incomparably greater than any ever produced by human agencies, and yet these results are but an embryo of what is to be.

That communication without wires to any point of the globe is practicable with such apparatus would need no demonstration, but through a discovery which I made I obtained absolute certitude. Popularly explained, it is exactly this: When we raise the voice and hear an echo in reply, we know that the sound of the voice must have reached a distant wall or boundary, and must have been reflected from the same. Exactly as the sound, so an electrical wave is reflected; and the same evidence which is afforded by an echo is offered by an electrical phenomenon known as a "stationary" wave — that is, a wave with fixed nodal and ventral regions. Instead of sending sound-vibrations toward a distant wall, I have sent electrical vibrations toward the remote boundaries of the earth, and instead of the wall the earth has replied. In place of an echo I have obtained a stationary electrical wave, — a wave reflected from afar.

Stationary waves in the earth mean something more than mere telegraphy without wires to any distance. They will enable us to attain many important specific results impossible otherwise. For instance, by their use we may produce at will, from a sending-station, an electrical effect in any particular region of the globe; we may determine the relative position or course of a moving object, such as a vessel at sea, the distance traversed by the same, or its speed; or we may send over the earth a wave of electricity traveling at any rate we desire, from the pace of a turtle up to lightning speed."

One of the experiments produced with a comparatively small machine of this kind is illustrated in Fig. 14. As no person could be anywhere in the vicinity when the display is going on, the picture was obtained by two successive processes, the image of Mr. Tesla's assistant being taken at one exposure and the electrical discharges photographed at another. Combined upon one plate they show relative sizes of the streams of light as compared with a human being. An idea of the force and volume of the sparks may be gained when it is stated that the thick-

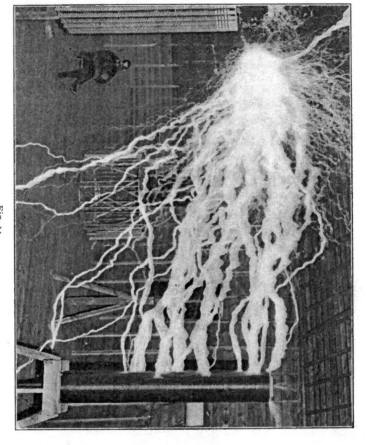

Fig. 14.

A TESLA EXPERIMENT IN ELECTRICAL DISCHARGES.
800 AMPERES, SPARKS 23 FEET LONG.
A ROAR LIKE NIAGARA.

est of them are about 23 feet long, and that a current of approximately 800 amperes is passing through the air. The roar of such a discharge can be heard several miles.

Since his return from Colorado in 1901 Tesla has begun the erection of commercial plants; but since two years nothing has been published about his work. It is understood that his wireless plant on Long Island is nearing completion. A photographic view of the same is shown in the illustration opposite page 49. The structure presents a curious appearance. As to the purpose for which the plant is designed, nothing has, as yet, been announced by Tesla. Recently, however, the "New York Sun" in an editorial authorized by him, stated that "the Tesla oscillator will deliver to the earth the shock that will be felt and recorded on its uttermost confines."

Tesla's Sun-Motors. —Fig. 15 and 16 illustrate other devices by the same inventor. These are called "apparatus for the utilization of radiant energy."

In Fig. 15, P is a plate exposed to rays, and P' a plate buried in the ground. C is a condenser, the plates of which should present as large a surface as possible, the inventor having ascertained the amount of energy conveyed to it per unit of time to be, under otherwise identical conditions, proportioned to the area exposed or nearly so. T and T' are terminals of condenser C. M a relay magnet or any other device capable of being actuated by an electric current. *d* may be composed of two very thin conducting plates placed in close proximity, and, either by reason of extreme flexibility, or from the character of their support, very mobile.

It will be seen that the magnet M, if energized and

de-energized, will actuate armature *a*, and, with a pawl and ratchet movement, turn, one step at a time, the wheel W. When the condenser C is charged to a certain potential the dielectric between the strips will break down, and the condenser discharge its accumulated energy through magnet M. When the strain on the dielectric has been relieved the strips *t t′* will resume their normal position.

The originator of this device says that "many useful applications of utilizing the radiations emanating from the sun, and many ways of carrying out the same, will at once suggest themselves."

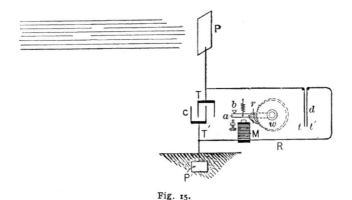

Fig. 15.

Application of Preceding to Telegraphy. — The application of this invention to telegraphy is suggested in Fig. 16, in which the source S of rays is a "Roentgen tube having but one terminal *k*, generally of aluminum, in the form of half a sphere with a plane polished surface on the front side from which the rays are thrown off." Interruption of the generation of the rays at differing intervals may

serve to produce long or short signals on the relay R.
The *t t'* of Fig. 15 takes, in Fig. 16, the form of a brush

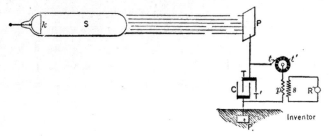

Fig. 16.

and segmented wheel. The condenser discharges are
stepped to higher intensities through induction coil, *p s.*

REESE LIBRARY
OF THE
UNIVERSITY
OF
CALIFORNIA

METHODS OF DR. SLABY.

In Mr. Kerr's work on Wireless Telegraphy is a foot-
note to the effect that Dr. Slaby of Charlottenburg, Germany, was present with Mr. Preece in the latter's Bristol
Channel experiments, and had repeated them before the
Emperor of Germany at Berlin. Presumably this refers
to the tests of 1892. Mr. Fahie has recorded that Dr.
Slaby was also present at a Bristol Channel experiment
made by Marconi on May 13th, 1899; and it seems to be
the opinion of the English writers that Dr. Slaby's successful trials in etheric transmission were all subsequent
to this latter visit to England.

Controversy Between Slaby and Marconi. — In a lecture
before the English Society of Arts delivered May 15th,
1901, Marconi quotes from a paper read by Slaby in
December, 1900, in which the latter, referring to the Marconi system, said: " The receiving wire was suspended,
insulated, and attached at the end of the coherer, the
other pole of which was connected to earth." Marconi, in
controverting this point, contended that in one of his
British patents, application for which was made on June 1,
1898, or two and one-half years previous to Slaby's statement, he (Marconi) said of his own device, "according
to this invention the conductor (aerial) is no longer
insulated, but is connected to earth through the primary of an induction coil, while the ends of the imperfect contact, or coherer, are connected to the ends of
the secondary of the connections passing through the
coherer."

Slaby's Multiplier. — Slaby has applied to his apparatus a coil of wire, designated a multiplier, which he claims acts as a resonator, being analogous to a hollow box placed under a tuning-fork. The Slaby adherents are careful to state that this device should not be confounded with an induction coil. Marconi, however, in the same paper before the Society of Arts, previously quoted, points out that it is no new thing to use a single coil of wire to produce self-induction.

Slaby's Achievements. — Immediately upon his return from England in May, 1899, after his attendance at the tests of the young Italian inventor, Dr. Slaby succeeded with his own apparatus in transmitting signals a distance of about thirteen miles ; and it has been claimed for him, although doubted by the friends of Marconi, that he has covered ninety miles from the shore to a moving vessel at sea. The German electrical papers say that in competitive tests the superiority of the German system has been to them satisfactorily proved ; but the Marconi adherents, properly enough, contend that a more convincing test of comparative merit might be had if each side were allowed to handle its own apparatus. In a newspaper interview in October, 1902, Marconi is reported as saying of Slaby, " He has adopted the main features of my system, the vertical wire, for instance. He introduces other variations which I consider detrimental. He has established a so-called system by which he has covered one-twentieth of the distance I have covered."

No United States Patents to Slaby. — Up to this writing it has not been possible to find any American patent of

the German scientist, but it is rumored that he has assigned American rights under his inventions to the General Electric Company of Germany.

The Slaby Theory. — Dr. Slaby has built his system on
the theory that if by means of a spark producer at its
lower end electrical oscillations are set up in a vertical
wire, the maximum amplitude of each oscillation will be at
the top point of the high wire.

Fig. 17 is a diagrammatic representation of one complete wave A E.   At B is its greatest rise, or its "crest."

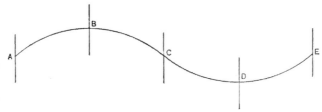

Fig. 17.

At D its point of extreme depression.   A, C, and E are
neutral points called nodes.   It follows, according to Dr.
Slaby, that a full wave from a transmitting station will be
just four times the length of the vertical wire which is set
in oscillation by the spark ; and also that if the antenna
of the receiver be put to earth its vibration will produce a
crest at its top corresponding to B, Fig. 17 ; and that in
consequence at the point of connection with the earth will
be nodes such as are indicated in Fig. 17, at A and C
and E.

Now, if a wire be carried, as in Fig. 18, from the node
A, the wave motion, of which B is the crest, will be prop-

agated along the wire A F, and provided the wire A F is
of exactly the same length as the wire A G, the crest B'
of the new wave will be formed at F, the point at which
Dr. Slaby attaches his coherer. He claims by this scheme
of connections that transmitted waves always affect the
coherer when at their maximums of potential. It is said
that those waves for which the earthed point A is not a
node will fail to be propagated along the wire A F, but

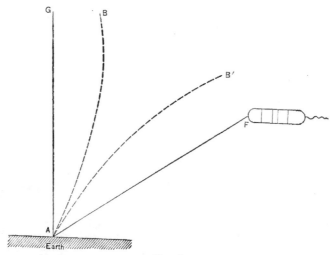

Fig. 18.

will be conducted directly into the ground, with the result
that only waves of a predetermined period will affect the
coherer, thus guarding against interception or interference;
or, again, that a number of differently constituted receiving
conductors, each adapted to receive an especial kind of
wave, may be branched from one receiving antenna, thus
making a wireless multiplex. There are, however, so far

as is known, no published results as to the number of circuits that may thus be operated, or the distance over which signals in groups may be transmitted.

Application of Multiplier. — While the author has not seen the application of the "multiplier" clearly shown, it may be assumed that the lower part of the antenna itself is in the form of a coil; that the path to the coherer, which must equal in length the antenna, is also in the form of a coil, but that these two coils are separate, and that there is between them no inductive action.

Slaby Coherer. — As a receiving device, Dr. Slaby uses steel balls lying loosely between aluminum plates. It is claimed, on the one hand, that this instrument is much more sensitive than the ordinary forms of what are called "permanent" coherers, such as tubes of carbon dust, but admitted on the other that it is not so sensitive as a delicately adjusted silver coherer; not, therefore, so well suited to extreme long distance transmission; and that it is not sufficiently diverse in its resistances to allow of working a relay; and consequently that a recording instrument which requires for its operation the local circuit of a relay cannot be used. To restate the advantages of the steel and aluminum coherer, it is the most sensitive form of "self-righting" coherer; and such being the case is best adapted of any to work at moderate distances where the signaling does not require a permanent record. The operator need have no difficulty in reading by sound from a telephone receiver, and can work faster than with an ink-marker; and any system which eliminates the tapper does away with a complicated and troublesome mechanism. The

Slaby receiver is apparently much easier of adjustment than can be any non-restoring coherer.

Dr. Slaby's circuits have inductances and capacities both at the transmitting and receiving ends. When he essays transatlantic signaling he will probably use a silver coherer. Then he may tune by getting the same product value in the combination of capacity and induction at each end of the transmission. Marconi does the same. Slaby's connections are somewhat different from those of his principal rival, but whether his net results will be greater remains for actual tests to determine.

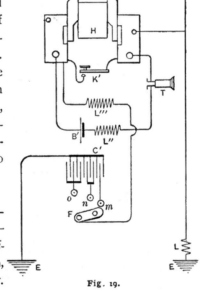

Fig. 19.

Mr. Collins's Description of Slaby System. — In the *Scientific American* of December 28th, 1901, is an article by Mr. A. F. Collins which gives a number of diagrams of Dr. Slaby's plans of connections, two of which, with a brief description, are by permission reproduced.

Referring to Figs. 19 and 20, D is the coherer (consisting of steel balls between aluminum plates). In Fig. 19

the path to ground from antenna A by way of coil L''' is in shunt with the coil L'', and both are in shunt with the key K', which while the operator is transmitting is kept closed to protect the coherer from strong waves. Induct-ance coil L, Fig. 19, is in tune with antenna A, and also in accord with waves from the distant station (see Fig. 20).

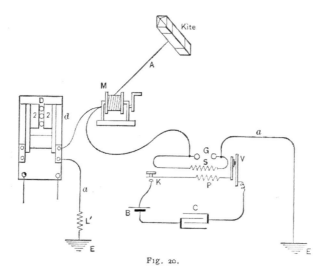

Fig. 20.

It is regulated by the adjustments of induction L''' and capacity C'. The method of changing the value of C' is shown by the position of switch-arm F and connections at *m, n* and *o*. Battery B' may be one dry cell; L'' acts as a choking coil. Fig. 20 represents the transmitting appa-ratus of Dr. Slaby, in which M is a multiplier and A with its terminating kite the wave-gate.

THE LODGE SYSTEM.

Fig. 21 is arranged as a typical diagram of Professor Lodge's ethereal transmitter. In the Lodge nomenclature it is called a "radiator." Three spark-gaps are in the series, viz.: the "starting," the "supply," and the "discharge." It is the assertion of the designer that by this multiplicity of gaps the oscillations are made more "persistent," i.e., not so soon "damped." He says that charges so communicated are left to oscillate free from any disturbance due to maintained connection with the source of electricity; and therefore "oscillate longer and more freely than when supplied by wires in the usual way." Another advantage is that the same emitter, inductance coils, and earth connection may conveniently be used as a part of the receiving apparatus. It will be seen that at the supply knobs the Ruhmkorff coil is always in absolute disconnection from the final discharge circuit. If now the receiving circuit shown in Figs. 22 or 23 be attached, as indicated by the dotted lines X X in Fig. 21 and the solid lines $x\,x$ in Figs. 22 and 23, and at the same time the discharge break be bridged out of circuit by a good conductor across it, the apparatus is ready for use as a receiver. The connections may be so arranged that one movement of a knife switch will change the device from transmitter to receiver, or, as the inventor would say, from "radiator to resonator."

Inductance Coils. — Fig. 24 shows the inductance coil of the receiver surrounded by a secondary winding, the two coils forming a step-up transformer to raise the potential of waves from a distant source.

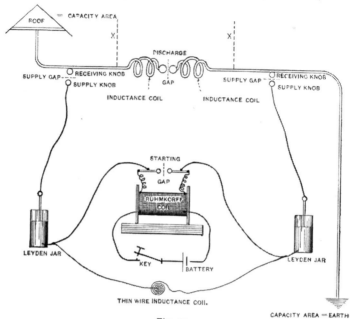

Fig. 21.

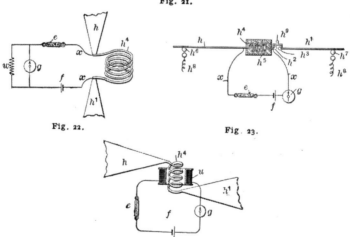

Fig. 22.

Fig. 23.

Fig. 24.

Capacity Areas. — Fig. 25 represents the form preferred by Professor Lodge for " capacity areas," "diverging cones with vertices adjoining and their larger areas spreading out into space." He says that this form combines low resistance with great electrostatic capacity.[1]

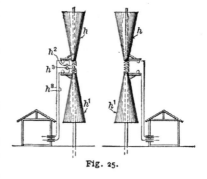

Fig. 25.

Supply Gap. — The action of the " supply gap" is to cause to be stored upon the " supply knob " a charge of electricity that is sufficiently powerful to cross the air space. A condenser is a similar storage of power, and supposedly much easier of exact adjustment.

In Professor Lodge's device there is in the local circuit as here shown no condenser, such as is found in the Marconi or Tesla systems, to build up the feeble waves arriving at the receiving end of a long distance transmission ; nor are there any choking coils to prevent the dissipation over the relay circuit of the charge that affects the coherer.[1]

[1] See Fig. 68, p. 177, Part IV.

WORK OF UNITED STATES WEATHER BUREAU.

Engagement of Specialist.—The United States Weather Bureau began, early in 1900, a systematic course of experimentation in Wireless Telegraphy, employing Professor Reginald A. Fessenden as a specialist. In a paper written by him in 1902, it was asserted that important advances had been made, one of which was overcoming largely the loss of energy experienced in other systems. He also declared that syntony was not safely selecting, but that he had discovered several methods which were. The following extract from the Fifth Annual Report of the Secretary of Agriculture is a generalization of the Government work up to the year 1901 :

"While there is much experimental work yet to be done before the present system is reliable for intership communication, or before any two systems can work within the same field without each rendering the other useless, such progress has been made by the government experimenters that, with no interference by private systems, stations can be successfully operated over at least one hundred and fifty miles of coast line; and they are now in operation on the North Carolina and Virginia coasts, and soon will be instituted between the Farallone Islands and the mainland, and Tatoosh Island and the mainland, on the Pacific coast."

Experimental Stations of U. S. Government. — Early in 1901 the Weather Bureau official installed Mr. Fessenden at Wier's Point, Roanoke Island, North Carolina ; and he has since made experimental transmissions across water to a station located about five miles west of Cape Hatteras, the distance between the two stations being almost exactly fifty miles. The following letters from the Weather Bureau staff have been given to the public :

DESCRIPTIVE.

MANTEO, ROANOKE ISLAND, N.C.,
April 4, 1902.

CHIEF UNITED STATES WEATHER BUREAU,
Washington, D.C.:

After working with Professor Fessenden's new receiver, between Hatteras and Roanoke, I would report as follows :

The receiver is positive in its action, and entirely and absolutely reliable. It is entirely different in nature and action from the coherer, and gives no false signals like the latter does.

I could get every single dot and dash made at Hatteras with the utmost clearness, and can receive with it at the same rate of speed as over an ordinary telegraph line. It is possible for any expert telegrapher to receive by it as fast as the key can be handled.

I have had no trouble in using the receiver except that due to bad sending at the other end, and even then could make out every single dot and dash, but could not read them.

The signals and messages were taken perfectly on the new receiver when, under the same conditions and connections, the coherer was tried and would not give a single dot.

Yours respectfully, LOUIS DORMAN,
Observer, Weather Bureau.

MANTEO, ROANOKE ISLAND, N.C.,
April 8, 1902.

Professor REGINALD A. FESSENDEN :

I would report that in the test made by Mr. Dorman, the following is a comparison of the amount of energy necessary to work the standard coherer and the receiver used by Mr. Dorman in the test referred to in his report :

Taken as our standard coherer one working well — i.e., giving good clear transmission of messages when attached to a single No. 18 wire five feet long, the sending wire being similar and of the same length, the spark-gap being one-eighth inch between slightly rounded points, and obtained from a coil capable of giving three-sixteenths inch spark between points when the distance between sending and receiving wires is forty-five feet, and both coherer and coil are resting on the surface of the ground — then the third message received by Mr. Dorman in the tests referred to in his report was received with one five-hundred-and-seventy-sixth of the least amount of energy required to work the standard coherer over the same distance, and with the same vertical and receiving wires used in each case, and with the coherer worked with a transformer with maximum efficiency ratio of transformation and circuit accurately tuned.

A. H. THIESSEN, *Assistant.*

Upon April 27, 1902, a series of tests were made from the Roanoke station before various Government officials, resulting in good transmission over fifty miles of a surface partly sea water and partly fresh water.

U. S. Government Opens Proposals For Wireless Telegraph in Alaska. — Upon May 6th, 1902, the Chief Signal Officer of the Weather Bureau opened proposals for establishing wireless telegraph systems in Alaska, over four different routes, as follows :

A.   Between Fort Davis and some point on Strait Island, a distance of ninety nautical miles.

B.   Between Fort Davis and Fort St. Michael's, a distance of one hundred and eight miles.

C.   From Rampart City to Winter Hours, a distance of one hundred and thirty-six miles.

D.   From Fort Gibbon to a point near Bates Rapids in the Tanana River, an air-line distance of one hundred and sixty-five miles.

The bidders were, Queen and Company of Philadelphia representing the Fessenden Apparatus ; The Marconi Company of England ; the owners of the Arco-Slaby system in Germany ; the American Wireless Telephone and Telegraph Co. of Philadelphia ; Foote, Pierson & Co. ; the DeForest Wireless Telegraph Company.

The proposals of the last four bidders were not considered, for the reason that they would not agree to install and work their systems for ten days prior to acceptance by the Government. Contracts were finally made with Queen and Company for the B route, one hundred and eight miles, with a rate of transmission guaranteed to be not less than twenty-five words per minute ; with the

Marconi Company for the D route, one hundred and sixty-five miles, with a guaranteed speed of twelve words per minute.

The Marconi Company departed from the specifications to the extent of demanding a royalty after the first year of $250 per annum upon each set of instruments; and also demanding one-half of any receipts for commercial telegraphy which might be received by the Government.

In accepting the contracts, both companies have agreed that unless their systems shall work every day without interruption the Government shall be exempt from payment. It was thought that both installations would be in working order by October, 1902.

Interview with Mr. Fessenden. — In an interview with a *New York Journal* correspondent, Mr. Fessenden said of his apparatus that he did not use any air transformer at the sending end; nor concentric cylinder for emitters and antennae, such as were employed by the Marconi Company; that he used capacity, but that it was arranged in a manner entirely different from that in other systems; that he did not employ a coherer or any form of imperfect contact; that his apparatus was of solid metal, and acted under a physical law entirely different from that which governs the receiving devices of Marconi. While the telephone was used as a recorder of signals, he said he could also get good service from a siphon recorder. He asserted that he had paid particular attention to selective and multiplex systems, and was well satisfied with the results in that direction. He believed that when a system of machine receiving was perfected it would be possible to transmit five hundred words per minute.

Lieutenant Beecher's Paper Before American Institute. ——
On May 28th, Lieutenant Beecher of the United States
Navy, who had been investigating the Fessenden system,
read a paper before the American Institute of Electrical
Engineers, in which he said that in some respects the Fessenden apparatus was more reliable than that devised by
other inventors. He emphasized the fact that one defect
of a telephonic receiving apparatus is the need of an
efficient calling-up signal ; and suggested that a coherer
might be used to receive the calling signal, and be afterward switched out and replaced by a telephone receiver.

On August 12th, 1902, there were issued to Mr. Fessenden thirteen patents on various methods, devices, and systems for signaling without wires.[1]

The First Two Patents. — In the first two patents of the series it is indicated that it was Mr. Fessenden's intention to devise a signaling system which would be more positive in its action at moderate distances than was the only receiving instrument known at that time, the coherer. He designated the transmitted vibrations which affect a coherer as "voltages," meaning electric currents of high potential in contradistinction to the "currents" of comparatively low potential which he employed.

His receiving organization is a tuned circuit which is always *closed*, and is thus differentiated from a coherer which may be called a normally open circuit. Hence his receiver is always receptive, always capable of being affected by waves; whereas for a portion of the time during which signals are being sent, the coherer is incapable of response. Another distinctive feature is the fact that the indications produced by the Fessenden receiving mechanism are dependent upon the total *amount of energy* emitted to form a signal, and not, as in the case of a coherer, dependent upon the *maximum* of the *voltage*.

In the description of that first invention it is explained that a single electromagnetic wave of the type used by the inventor "will have produced its impulses before the receiver employed will have made an appreciable motion";

---

[1] Many of these devices are described as "Apparatus" in Part IV., and a full list of them is a portion of Part II., under "Inventors and Inventions."

but by using a source of sustained radiation at the sending end the effect of the waves is cumulative ; and since the receiver is constantly receptive, the effects added together from a number of waves serve to produce appreciable indications. Repeating the foregoing statements in other words, the appliances are adapted to produce at the sending station electromagnetic waves of comparatively low frequency and low potential, but to sustain as much as possible the oscillations from each impulse, and at the receiving station to use a wave-responsive-device upon a closed circuit tuned to the same frequency as the sending organization, which would be sufficiently affected by the cumulative effect of a number of waves as to produce observable mechanical movements.

After the declarations of principles, which constitute considerable portions of his first two patents, there appeared in successive inventions two different forms of radiating wave-gates.[1]

Third Patent for a " System." — Next in order is a " system." Its objects are to provide suitable means for

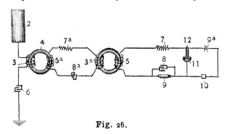

Fig. 26.

raising the voltage at the receiving station by a transformer; to increase the number of oscillations in the sending conductor during its discharging period ; and to improve localization by so tuning the receiving apparatus that it will respond solely to waves

[1] See detailed description in Part IV.

of one periodicity. Referring to Fig. 26, the inventor
says that a feature (indicated at 6) is the addition of a
capacity to the sending conductor in connection with
a transformer at the receiving station for raising the voltage in the secondary circuit ; that another feature is the
capacity (8) placed in shunt with the coherer (9) ; still
another, an opposing source of voltage (12–11) bridged
across the secondary circuit and presenting a counter electromotive force to the local battery while the coherer is in
operation. The PRINCIPAL ADVANTAGE claimed seems to
be the improvement in selection, due to the use of a plurality of TUNED CIRCUITS.

Quoting the inventor's own words :

Waves of One Periodicity Subject to Interference. —
On account of the fact that it is preferable to use sending
conductors having large capacity, or large capacity and
self-induction, and that in these cases the curve of resonance is broadened, it has heretofore been impossible to
make the receivers respond solely to waves of one periodicity, as other periodicities, if above a certain power, will
affect the receivers.

**Perfect Resonance Attained by Plurality of Conduc-
tors.** — By constructing the sending conductor so the oscillations for each total discharge are increased, and by
employing at the receiving station two or more tuned circuits, a very perfect resonance or tuning between the
stations can be attained.

**Effects from One-Tuned Circuit and Two-Tuned Cir-
cuits.** — With a one-tuned circuit at the receiving station
and with sending conductors permitting a rapid radiation

at the sending station, electrostatic and hysteresis effects
become very prominent, and the great self-inductance
desirable for sharp resonance cannot be attained. By
employing at the receiving end two tuned circuits, the first
consisting of the receiving conductor and the other secondary to the first, the relative inductance may be greater in
the secondary than in the primary circuit of the receiving conductor or the sending conductor, in which latter,

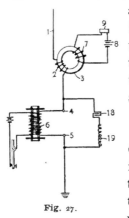

as before explained, the capacity
is preferably a dominant factor of
tuning, and the electrical effect in
the secondary will occur only when
the periods are very closely the
same.

**An Invention in Wireless Teleph-
ony.** — In an application for a patent
filed September 28th, 1901, part of
the subject matter had reference to
telephoning without wires. The
method is illustrated in Fig. 27, in

Fig. 27.

which 9 is a transmitting telephone modifying by means
of battery 8, coil 7 and core 3, the impulses imparted to
wave-gate 1.

Invention for Localization of Signals. — An arrangement for the more distinct localization of signals than can
be obtained from one set of tuned apparatus is shown in
Fig. 28, in which 1^a and 2^a are emitting wave-gates tuned
to different periodicities, and 6^a and 7^a are receiving antennae respectively corresponding in frequency to 1^a and
2^a, and consequently the armature 16 which represents the

means for mechanical movement at the receiving station responds "only to the combined action of waves or impulses corresponding in period and in other characteristics to those generated" by the *combined* action of 1ª and 2ª.

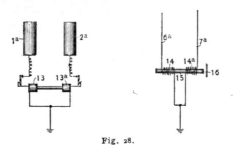

Fig. 28.

Reference is made to Part IV., wherein are described inventions by Mr. Fessenden of,

1. Means "to provide for the MAINTENANCE of a CERTAIN DEFINITE RELATION BETWEEN the RESISTANCE and CAPACITY of the sending mechanism, regardless of the POTENTIAL employed.

2. A WAVE-RESPONSIVE-DEVICE, consisting of a conductor having small heat capacity and low resistance.

3. An appliance adapted to make a highly CONDUCTIVE WAVE PATH OVER THE EARTH for some distance, from the sending end and receiving wave-gates respectively. This is denominated by the inventor a "wave-chute."

4. An arrangement for PRODUCING VISIBLE INTERPRETABLE CHARACTERS on a strip or film by a PHOTOGRAPHIC process, and for developing and fixing the same.

Fessenden's Selective System. — Another invention is a system of selection whereby each of a number of stations has a tune or period of resonance proper to itself, as each Western Union Telegraph station has, where several stations work upon one wire, its particular letter or combination of letters for a "call." In this system, part of the sending mechanism is a key,[1] constructed with a number of different contacts which are the terminals of differently tuned circuits. The connections are normally made so that their period of resonance is that allotted to each station ; but any station may call and exchange signals with any other station by first putting itself in resonance with the one with which it desired to communicate.

Fessenden Signaling System of July, 1902 (Fig. 29). — For the Fessenden patent No. 706,745, application was made July 1, 1902. It is for a "system," apparently the final result of the researches and experiments made by the inventor for the Government. The drawings of the patent comprise five illustrations, the second, third, fourth, and fifth figures being forms of apparatus at the receiving station which are modifications of that shown in the first figure. As it is presumable that the initial illustration is the preferred one, it has been selected for description, and reproduced here as Fig. 29.

Transmitter. — Quoting from the patent specification, "The form of apparatus shown in Fig. 29 consists at the sending station of a radiating conductor (1) connected to one terminal of the spark-gap, the opposite terminal being grounded ; a generator (A) and a local tuned circuit con-

---

[1] See Figs. 74, 75, and 76 in Part IV., p. 187.

taining a capacity (12) in parallel with the sending conductor for the purpose of prolonging the radiation.

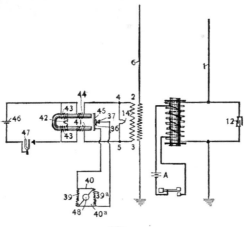

Fig. 29.

Receiver. — At the receiving end is employed a current-operated wave-responsive-device[1] in a closed tuned circuit (2, 3, 4, 5) energized by the receiving conductor (6) containing the primary of a transformer.

Circuit. — The circuit 2, 3, 4, 5, which is a secondary circuit, is tuned to the frequency of the electromagnetic waves, is preferably of low resistance, and has a larger ratio of inductance to capacity than that of the receiving conductor. This is for the purpose of protecting the receiver from foreign electrical disturbances.

Indicating Mechanism. — " Any suitable form of indicating mechanism, such as a telephone or galvanometer, may be employed. A differentially-wound indicating mechan-

---

[1] See Fig. 59, p. 167, Part IV.

ism, such as the differentially-wound telephone 41, is desirable for many purposes, and has one circuit connected
across the receiver 14.   A resistance 42, preferably formed
by a loop similar to the receiver 14, is arranged in one of
the circuits of the differential instrument, the receiver 14
being in the other circuit, so that the circuits are balanced.
Coils 43 and 44 are oppositely wound, and the two circuits
being balanced there is normally no appreciable effect on
the diaphragm 45.   The source of voltage, 46, and tuning-
fork, 47, are used to produce intermittent currents in the
differential circuits, and, as mentioned above, there is normally no effect.   When an electromagnetic wave causes a
current to pass through the loop 14, thereby raising its resistance, the current in circuits containing the coils 44 of
the differential instrument is weakened, and the circuits
being out of balance an indication is produced by the
instrument.

**Generation may be Made Continuous Instead of Intermit-
tent.** — "When it is not desired to use an intermittent current, — as, for example, when the receiving mechanism is
tuned mechanically to a given note for selective purposes,
— the circuit including the generator is made continuous,
as by wedging the prongs of the tuning-fork, or in any
other suitable manner.

Operation. — "When a train of waves is radiated from
the sending station and received by the receiving conductor,
it causes currents to flow through the receiver, 14,[1] heat-
ing it up, thereby changing its resistance.   The resistance
of the differential circuit containing the receiver is therefore increased, the current therein reduced, and sound produced by the telephone.

[1] See Fig. 59, p. 167, Part IV.

Transformer. — "The transformer is here shown as a
step-down transformer, as this form has advantages when
used in connection with current-operated receivers of very
low resistance ; but step-up transformers may be used."

Means of Amplifying Indications. — "As a means of
amplifying the indications, I prefer to use a local microphonic circuit, as shown in Fig. 29, where a small carbon
block, 36, is attached to the diaphragm of the differential
telephone, 41, and a carbon point, 37, bears lightly thereon.
A local battery generates a current which passes continuously through the microphonic contact and a bridge consisting of the arms, 39 39^a and 40 40^a, and a siphon
recorder, 48. The arms of the bridge are balanced as
regards ohmic resistance. Hence for all steady or slowly
varying currents no portion of the current passes through
the siphon recorder. The arms 39 39^a have, however, very
high self-induction, and the arms 40 40^a very low self-induction, and both are of low resistance. On any sudden
change of current, such as will be produced by the motion
of the diaphragm on the receipt of a signal, the suddenly
varying current cannot flow through the arms 39 39^a, but
will flow through the arms 40 40^a and the siphon recorder,
48, thereby producing an amplified indication.

Definitions and Uses of Closed and Open Circuits. — " The
local circuit thus formed is a closed circuit, and is to be
differentiated from the open local circuits employed in connection with the coherer. An alternating-current circuit
may be closed through a resistance, an inductance, or a
capacity ; and since even the insulated ends of a circuit

will always have some capacity relative to each other, it
follows that all alternating-current circuits are theoretically
closed. What is meant, therefore, by a 'closed alternating-
current circuit,' is a circuit in which the current is relatively large for a small impressed voltage in the circuit, —
i.e., the circuit is one of low virtual resistance as compared
with a coherer. By an 'unclosed' or 'open' circuit is
meant one in which the current is relatively small or neg-
ligible for a small impressed voltage, — i.e., one whose
virtual resistance is high. Where a current-actuated wave-
responsive-device is employed, a closed circuit should also
be employed to obtain a large effective current to actuate
said-device. Where a voltage-actuated device, such as a
coherer, is employed and a large effective difference of
potential is required, an open circuit, as defined above,
should be used. This is especially important, because
while a resonant rise of voltage may be obtained in an open
circuit, a large resonant rise of current is possible only in
a closed circuit of low ohmic resistance used in connection
with a source of maintained radiation. It will be evident
that according to this definition of closed and unclosed
tuned circuits, in many cases the sending or receiving conductor would come under the head of a 'closed tuned
circuit,' especially when having large capacity and low inductance ; but where reference is made herein to a 'closed
tuned circuit' a sending or receiving conductor is not
meant. It is characteristic of these closed tuned circuits
that they have a peculiar advantage when used in connection with the form of receiver in that such circuits act to
prevent the burning out of the receivers by electrical disturbances produced by lightning discharges. They also
permit of the employment of more sensitive current-actu-

ated wave-responsive-devices. They also permit of step-
down transformers being used, instead of step-up, thus
enabling practically all of the energy of the waves to be
utilized, and giving sufficient inductance with small length
of wire."

Small Voltages Characteristic of Fessenden Circuits. —
" It is especially characteristic of my invention — i.e., the
use of closed tuned circuits in connection with current-
actuated wave-responsive-devices as distinguished from
open tuned circuits and voltage-actuated wave-responsive-
devices — that in my construction the voltages in the
receiving circuit are kept small, and hence practically all
the energy received from the electromagnetic waves is
employed affecting the receiver, and hence indications can
be produced by an amount of energy which is an extremely
small fraction of that necessary when open tuned circuits
and voltage-actuated wave-responsive-devices are employed.

Practical Test of Transmission. — " Thus since the capacity of a coherer is small, a small amount of energy is
sufficient to raise it by itself to a breakdown voltage ; but
in operation it is connected to a circuit having several
hundred times the capacity ; and as this circuit must be
raised to practically the same potential as the coherer, the
efficiency of working is low — as, for example, with closed
tuned circuits and a receiver, messages at the rate of thirty
words per minute were sent and received over a distance
of fifty miles, (i.e., from Cape Hatteras to Roanoke Island,)
using a spark one thirty-second ($\frac{1}{32}$) of an inch long at the
sending end. When a coherer and an open tuned circuit
were used under the same circumstances, the spark length

had to be increased to five and one-half inches before any messages could be received. The energies in the two cases were approximately in the ratio of one to forty thousand.

Definition of Current-Operated Wave-Responsive-Device. — " By the term ' current-operated wave-responsive-devices ' as used herein and by me generally is meant wave-responsive-devices having all their contacts good contacts, and operated by currents produced by electromagnetic waves. They are hence to be distinguished from wave-responsive-devices depending for operation upon varying contact resistance."

EHRET'S DEVICE.

Fig. 30. — From the multitude of inventions contributing to wireless telegraphy not familiar to the public, one is selected here as representative of recent advances in this art, although the author has not had opportunity from the data of results or from knowledge of experimental demonstrations, to judge of its relative importance. The invention is described in United States Letters Patent No. 699,158, dated May 6, 1902, and issued to Cornelius D. Ehret of Washington, D.C. One of the striking features of this patent is its comprehensive brevity. All of the drawings are shown as Fig. 30. The figure I extending across the top of the page gives a detailed representation, and the other six drawings illustrate modifications of the first organization. While the space is well filled, it will be noted that there is neither confusion of line nor the omission of any necessary detail. The description of the invention is equally brief, about one thousand words sufficing to explain seven different schemes of connections.

Recording Mechanism. — In the figure at the top of the page, S may represent a register which records dots and dashes in ink upon paper tape, and is operated whenever battery B″ is put on a closed circuit by reason of retractile spring 7 pulling lever 4 against contact 5. When the apparatus is at rest, lever 4 is held against stop 6.

Differential Relay (R). — It will be noted that relay R has wound *differentially* about its core 3 two coils *f* and *g*; and consequently if electric currents of the *same strength*

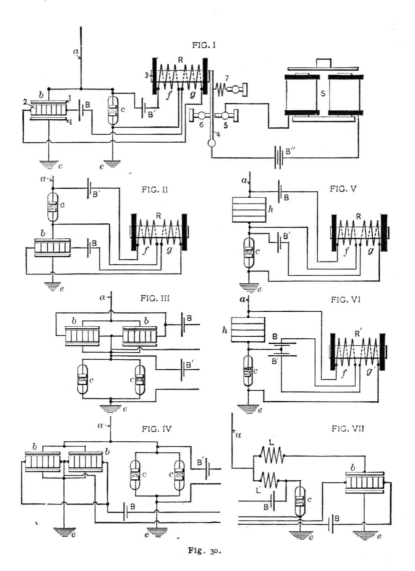

Fig. 30.

and direction be sent through them simultaneously the effect on core 3 is nil.

Core (3). — Core 3 in itself, without the aid of current effect, is slightly magnetic; and battery B and coil *g* are so arranged that their influence upon core 3 is to induce in it a magnetism of the same polarity as that already existing, and so to increase the magnetic effect.

Coherer (c). — On the other hand, battery B′ and the winding of coil *f* are arranged to work in opposition to coil *g* and battery B. *c* is the usual filings coherer which, under the influence of Hertzian waves, *decreases* in resistance. It is a part of the same circuit which includes battery B′ and coil *f*.

Anti-Coherer (2). — 2 is a device called an anti-coherer, and may consist of tin-foil glued to a glass plate, as in a mirror, and with slits cut across the metal as indicated in the drawing. The effect of etheric impulses upon an anti-coherer is to *increase* its resistance. The anti-coherer 2 is a part of the same circuit which includes battery B and coil *g*.[1]

Operation. — When, therefore, waves from a distant source impinge upon antenna *a* circuit 2 B *g* which tends to hold lever 4 against stop 6 is greatly weakened; and circuit *c* B′ *f* which tends to repel the armature of lever 4 is made much stronger. Consequently the magnetic effect in core 3 is neutralized, and spring 7 draws lever 4 against contact 5, thus actuating S. Tapping the coherer *c* during

[1] See p. 154, Part IV., in connection with "anti-coherers."

the absence of wave effect opens circuit c B$'$ f, and at the same instant anti-coherer 2 regains its normal conductivity and the armature 4 is again attracted to core 3.

Advantages. —— Presumably the advantages attained by this plan of connection are, first, greater certainty of action ; second, a closer adjustment ; third, less self-inductive influence in the receiving relay, and consequently its quicker action.

THE DEFOREST SYSTEM.

Officials connected with the DeForest system claim the best record for accurate service during the naval maneuvers which took place off the New England coast in the summer of 1902. The principal feature of their system is the wave-responsive-device, which is designated by its inventors a "responder." This instrument is described as an anti-coherer in Part IV., and is illustrated by Fig. 49. In connection with transmitters the DeForest system is further described in the same division.

WIRELESS TRANSMISSION OVERLAND.

There have been no records available of successful experiments in this country with wireless telegraphy overland, but in the Marconi article in the *Century Magazine*, March, 1902, the inventor expressed the belief that the possibilities for inland wireless telegraphy are limited to one thousand miles. The Federal Wireless Telephone Company of New York has frequently advertised that it was about to open communication between Baltimore and Washington, a distance of forty miles, but there is no record of a test for even so far. In newspaper interviews Mr. Fessenden is reported as saying that his apparatus was about to be tested between Annapolis and Washington, after which he should try a circuit from Chicago to New York; but directly after these interviews Lieutenant Beecher of the United States Navy declared, in a paper before the American Institute of Electrical Engineers on May 28, that he believed the field of wireless telegraphy to be limited to the ocean ; and Lieutenant Beecher is supposed to be well acquainted with the Fessenden apparatus.

Overland Contracts in Alaska. — The chief signal officer of the United States Weather Bureau has contracted with the Marconi Company for a circuit of one hundred and sixty-five miles in an air-line from Bates Rapids in the interior of Alaska to Fort Gibbon near the sea-coast. According to the map this must be almost entirely overland, and presenting rather difficult conditions at that.

NEW MARCONI RECEIVER.

In a lecture in London on June 13, 1902, Mr. Marconi reported that he had invented a receiver sufficiently sensitive to allow of a transmission at the rate of thirty words per minute.[1]

GUARINI'S REPEATER.

An Italian scientist, Signor Guarini, seems to have been partially successful in designing a wireless-telegraph-repeater, its function being to pick up signals at a certain distance and relay them onward with renewed strength.

WIRELESS TELEPHONY.

Telephoning without wires has not gained by the great developments in its sister-art. Mr. A. F. Collins, an American, reports that he has heard faint tones at a distance of three miles through what he terms the " earth-bound-ether ; " but he does not make public his methods

[1] See Fig. 58 and accompanying description in Part IV., p. 165.

or devices. Telephonic waves are readily propagated through space, but the difficulty is to confine them to an intended recipient. Mr. Collins admits that the problem of making wireless telephony selective is one calculated to discourage the most sanguine investigator. The inventions of Professor Pupin have decreased the first cost of telephone equipment and increased the distance of good transmission. Perhaps a multiplex transmission over *one small* copper wire connecting the two points will eventually be the best device for selective telephony.

PRACTICABILITY.

Notwithstanding the great mass of positive evidence, there are many conservative people who doubt that wireless telegraphy is or will be an art commercially practicable. Public exhibitions have so often proved disappointing that a great deal of disparaging testimony has circulated. Also, there has lately become prominent the curious fact that sunlight so interferes with wireless service, that to overcome its effect, the energy necessary for transmission during daylight must be several times that needed for the same service at night; and despite previous statements that the earth's curvature does not interfere with space signalling, it now appears that for equal distances there would be needed over a flat surface only one-third of the energy now required; but these facts only indicate that more power must be applied than was at first thought needful. Always the public is looking for *revolution* in an art and almost always, after the original discovery, progress is made by a process of *evolution* from discoveries already made. It may with comparative safety be predicted that this art, as have most others, will develop with step by step movements consisting mainly in the careful and thorough application of comparatively small yet essential details, the principles of which are already well understood, although their aggregate importance may not now be fully realized.

To illustrate the foregoing by analogies, the two most essential features in the development of wire telegraphy have been the adoptions of screw-glass insulators and of hard-drawn copper conductors; yet copper soft-drawn was about the first thing tried (being soon abandoned for iron), and the glass insulator at first without the screw threads to fasten it to brackets or pins has been in use from the outset. When the smooth-bore glass sprung off the pin, as it often did, the wire lay against the wood-work and lost part of its current. Again hard-drawn copper was first used in the form of thin wires, and although it has been known for more than a century that a telegraph circuit may by the use of large wires be operated to proportionally longer distances than by small ones, many years elapsed before the telegraph companies seemed to realize that fact. If we review telephone progress, it will be found that one of its important steps, the transposition of circuits to prevent cross-talk, was fully set forth twenty years ago;* but that it was ten years after that before such transposition was systematized and made effective.

Professor Fleming of the Marconi Company has recently reviewed the whole art of wireless telegraphy. He has positively asserted that communications may be carried on between stations three thousand miles apart, and Professor Fleming has had every opportunity by experiment and observation upon which to base such an assertion.

* In U. S. Patent to author, No. 240776, filed Sept. 28, 1880.

MAXWELL   HERTZ

        MARCONI

BRANLY   LODGE

PART II.

INVENTORS AND INVENTIONS.

A CURIOUS feature in the record of Wireless Telegraphy is the fact that while the press and public were hailing Mr. Marconi as the only inventor of all that pertained to the system by which he signaled across the ocean, the name of an equally important patentee was hardly mentioned.

It is true that Professor Silvanus Thompson, an English electrician of repute, had once or twice been quoted in newspaper paragraphs as saying that the Marconi system was a direct infringement upon American patents granted to Professor Lodge; but the representatives of the Marconi Company disparaged the statement, declaring that Marconi had taken out eleven United States patents and Lodge but one.

A careful search, including all of the year 1902, reveals only ten patents issued to Marconi. One of these, however, has been reissued, and may have been counted in addition. On the other hand, at the date of the transatlantic transmission by Marconi there had been on record for several months the award of very important claims to Professor Lodge by the most competent tribunal in the world, the United States Patent Office.

It is not purposed to make this writing controversial, much less to belittle Marconi's achievements. That in faith in himself and his project, in force of character and ability to inspire confidence in others, he holds very high rank, is indisputable ; moreover, he must be recognized as the maker of an epoch. At the same time, the historian of this art would be remiss who did not endeavor so to sift the evidence as to apportion to the man upon the pedestal only his due, to the end that to other contributors might come rightful credit.

In his " Evolution of the Electric Incandescent Lamp," the late Franklin Leonard Pope opens the preface of his first edition with an essay upon the tendency of an unthinking public to bestow its praise for a new invention upon but one person. Mr. Pope, in 1889, when this was written, was a recognized authority on patent matters, as well as one of the foremost electrical engineers. He said :

"The outcome of a race of diligence between two independent but equally meritorious inventors is perhaps as often as otherwise determined by chance or accident. In this respect it may not inaptly be compared to the result of a horse-race in which the fortunate winner carries off, not only all the honors, but the purse as well, although his nose may have passed under the wire barely an inch in advance of some of his no less deserving competitors. It is a matter of common observation that when the fullness of time arrives the discovery or invention for which the world has been waiting is certain to be made. The critical student of affairs perceives that however wonderful or however unexpected that invention may appear, it is seldom that it is not found to be a necessary sequence of a long series of other discoveries and inventions which have preceded it. Even in those rare cases in which an improvement of indisputable novelty and originality is made known to the industrial world, it is scarcely ever sufficiently perfected in its details to be capable of practical use until it has been worked upon and improved by many hands and many minds.

" It has always been the way of the world to consider every such invention, especially when of a character to appeal to the minds of the masses, or to identify itself closely with the everyday life of the community, as the work of some particular individual, who, as it were by common consent, is regarded as its sole originator and contriver, and upon him fame, honor and

wealth are lavished without stint, in childlike unconsciousness of the universal truth that inventions of this character are not made, but grow; that they are not the fruit of momentary inspiration, but on the contrary are the inevitable results which, from time to time, mark the slow but constant progress of scientific and industrial evolution."

Another phase of popular treatment is reaction, which often changes from adulation to indifference or positive condemnation. Sinister congratulations from the Anglo-American Cable Company were the immediate fruits of Marconi's triumph in Newfoundland, and shortly afterwards a meeting of the French Academy of Science indulged in hostile criticism. The speakers at that meeting contended that documentary evidence showed "that credit for the invention of a wireless telegraph is due first to Feddersen and Maxwell of England, then to Hertz of Germany, but principally to Professor Branly, a Frenchman, who invented the coherer; then to Professor Lodge of England and Professor Popoff of Russia. Finally it was pointed out that neither the French army nor the German navy was using the Marconi system."

Mr. Pope, in his "Evolution of the Electric Incandescent Lamp," further says: "It is particularly desirable that the line of demarcation between the improvements which unquestionably involve invention, and those which really exhibit nothing beyond an unusually high order of mechanical or engineering skill, should be more distinctly defined. The question at best is a difficult one; perhaps in its application to individual cases the most difficult one which the courts, sitting in patent cases, are ever called upon to determine."

Probably invention will be always more or less intangible, and thus difficult of exact definition. Precedent, however, has firmly established the principle that inventive genius must be something more than the manifestation of such technical knowledge and skill as might reasonably be expected of a person trained in any art. The inventor must be the fortunate one who has moments of happy inspiration leading to results never realized by hundreds of faithful, patient plodders, straining to reach the same goal. Like the true poet or artist, the inventor is born, not made. As a practical test, in the case of an alleged invention, the question might be raised whether, with well-known appliances and principles and furnished with the same facilities as were at the disposal of the applicant for a monopoly, a hundred skilled mechanics or engineers could have achieved the same result. If not, and if the applicant has discovered new principles or devised novel appliances, then he has made a true invention. Of a number of necessary qualifications the most important is that originality which a thorough training in any one line tends to deaden.

So far as the territory of the United States is concerned, the claims allowed in a patent are to some extent a warrant of monopoly to the inventor. The burden lies with the litigant opposing the patentee to show either that the Patent Office did not possess all the information bearing on the matter, or that possessing such information the Office erred. It has become the practice of examiners to give the applicant considerable latitude ; and as at that first tribunal there is no opposing counsel to break down the case, it often happens that if a patent is subsequently contested before a court it is pronounced invalid.

In the report of the Commissioner of Patents for 1892 appears the statement that,

"Of 988 court cases reported in the Official Gazette of the Patent Office between 1886 and 1892 wherein patents were in litigation, 436 patents were sustained and 522 were declared invalid in whole or in part. Of the number declared invalid, 428 were by reason of some fault in the Patent Office, and 124 on account of evidence brought to light of which the Office had no knowledge before granting the patents."

Again he says : "Approaching the subject from another side, I am furnished with the result of examinations as to the validity of the claims in ten patents taken at random where searches in this office were made by a well known law-firm. These patents contain fifty claims, of which thirty-five were considered and were reported to be old."

Patent Law from the point of view of an English scientist is discussed by Professor Lodge, in his " Signalling Through Space Without Wires," as follows :

"In the present state of the law in this country it appears to be necessary for a scientific man whose investigations may have any practical bearing, to refrain from communicating his work to any scientific society, or publishing it in any journal, until he has registered it and paid a fee to the Government under the so-called Patent Law. This unfortunate system is well calculated to prevent scientific men in general from giving any attention to practical applications, and to deter them from any attempt to make their researches useful to the community. If a scientific worker publishes in the natural way, no one has any right in the thing published. It is given away, and lies useless, for no one will care to expend capital upon a thing over which he has no effective control. In this case practical developments generally wait until some outsider steps in and either patents some slight addition or modification, or else, as sometimes happens, patents the whole thing with some slight addition.

" If a scientific worker refrains from publishing and himself takes out a patent, there are innumerable troubles and possible litigation ahead of him, — at least if the thing turns out at all remunerative ; but the possibility is, that in his otherwise occupied hands it will not so turn out until the period of his patent right has expired.

" Pending a much-to-be-desired emendation of the law, whereby the courts can take cognizance of discoveries or fundamental steps in an invention communicated to and officially dated by a responsible scientific society, and can thereafter award to the discoverer such due and moderate recompense as shall seem appropriate when a great industry has risen on the basis of that same discovery or fundamental invention ; pending this much-to-be-desired modification of the law, it appears to be necessary to go through the inappropriate and repulsive form of registering a claim to an attempt at monopoly. The instinct of the scientific worker is to publish everything, to hope that any useful aspect of it may be as quickly as possible utilized, and to trust to the instinct for fair play that he shall not be the loser when the thing becomes commercially profitable. To grant him a monopoly is to grant him more than a doubtful boon; to grant him the privilege of fighting for his monopoly is to grant him a pernicious privilege which will sap his energy, waste his time, and destroy his power of future production."

THE CHAIN OF INVENTION.

Reference to Professor Dolbear's patent printed in the appendix reveals a well defined transmission of electric waves without wires in 1882; and the historical part of this work records instances of wireless signaling nearly half a century before that date. (See Achievement.)

Upon May 23rd, 1885, Mr. Thomas A. Edison filed an application for a United States Patent, which was finally issued upon December 29th, 1891, numbered 465,971. It differs from Dolbear's organization in that a key is used to send out signals instead of a telephone to transmit words. The receiving apparatus may be a telephone or other recording apparatus. The Edison specification sets forth all the uses to which a wireless telegraph may be put, such as transmitting signals from a shore to moving vessels, signalling across bodies of water in lieu of using submarine cables; and as well across land spaces. It provides for the earth's curvature by interposing along a route condensing surfaces so arranged that there shall be always a clear air space between any surface and its immediate neighboring ones in either direction.

It is reported that this patent has been purchased by the Marconi interests. It has five years to run. The first claim is as follows :

"CLAIM I. Means for signalling between stations separated from each other, consisting of an elevated condensing surface, or body at each station, a transmitter operatively connected to one of said condensing surfaces for varying its electrical tension in conformity to the signal to be transmitted and thereby correspondingly varying the tension of the other condensing surface; and a signal receiver operatively connected to said other condensing surface substantially as described.

CLAIM 2 adds to the combination a condensing surface at such elevation that a straight line between said surfaces and the terminal surfaces will avoid the curvature of the earth's surface. Claim 3 adds an induction transmitter. Claim 4 brings in the secondary and the primary of an induction coil, a transmitting key, and a telephone receiver. Claim 5 has a new combination of the elements previously noted."

All of these earlier transmissions, however, are supposed to have been due to the propagation through space of magnetic lines of force, or magnetic waves. The period of ethereal transmission dates from the discoveries in 1886 of Professor Hertz, of Carlsruhe, Germany, who found that a disruptive discharge of electricity across a spark-gap produced a wave motion essentially different from the magnetic movement. His receiver of these waves was a piece of wire so bent as to bring its ends almost together. (Fig. 48.) In the little space between the ends of the bent wire he detected a response to the discharges from a Ruhmkorff coil. These responses were in the form of minute sparks. Between the spark-gap of the machine and the bent wire there was no tangible conductor of any kind. The adjective "Hertzian" in the patents of Lodge and of Marconi are acknowledgements to the physicist of Carlsruhe.

Contemporaneously with the work of Hertz, Professor Calzecchi-Onesti, an Italian scientist, devised apparatus consisting of a glass tube containing metal filings, and revoluble on an axis. He found that a group of filings which, under normal conditions, gave a very great resistance to an electric current, became a good conductor if subjected to the secondary impulse that occurs when an electric wire circuit is broken ; but if, after the discharge had ceased, the glass tube containing the filings was turned over in such a way as to disarrange them, the filings became again a highly resistant mass.

Branly's Discovery, 1891. — In 1891 Professor Branly of the Catholic Institute of Paris, made the discovery that electric sparks across an air-gap caused filings to cohere,

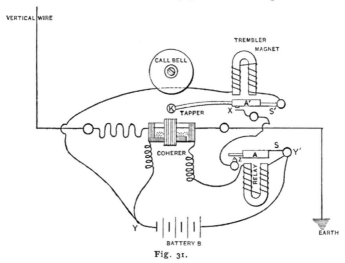

Fig. 31.

and also that a shock or tap imparted to the tube served to decohere them. The coherer has since been commonly called the "Branly tube." It would seem, however, that in the matter of a tube of filings, Professor Onesti is more properly entitled to the honor of being the originator.

Popoff's Early Devices. — In April, 1895, Professor A. Popoff, of the Cronstadt Torpedo School, described to the Russian Physico-Chemical Society of St. Petersburg a device which he was using in connection with the study of atmospheric electricity, and in December of the same year he said in a note to that Society that he hoped to make his apparatus applicable to telegraphic signaling.

Description of Fig. 31. — There is shown in Fig. 31 the organization used by Popoff. The line in the diagram marked " vertical wire" was his exploring antenna for atmospheric electrical manifestations. It may be explained that the parts represented as separated at the point X are in contact when the apparatus is at rest. When waves from a distant point impinge upon the vertical wire they pass through the coherer to earth, changing the coherer from an insulating path to a conducting one. This change causes a current to flow from battery B through the relay. The relay magnet, thus becoming energized, pulls down armature A which has been held upward by spring S, making contact at Z. There results a division of current at Y and Y', by which the trembler magnet is caused to pull upward the armature A' and sound an alarm on the call-bell. This upward movement of A' destroys the contact at X, and spring S' draws down A', the momentum imparted to knob K serving to make it tap the coherer.

Dr. Lodge as a Patentee. — From the allowed claims of his United States patents, Dr. Lodge would seem to constitute the most important link in the chain of inventors of wireless telegraphy. An inspection of his claims shows that he is recognized as the originator of the " emitter," the single conducting body from which waves are sent into

space ; of the metal shield which protects the receiving
apparatus from damage or from operation by the transmitter at the same station with it ; of the automatic means
of decohering the trembler in a local circuit ; of the combination with a coherer and battery of a telegraphic
receiving instrument ; and finally of the scheme of syntonizing which attunes by adjustments of inductance and
capacity.

Professor Lodge's system has already been explained.
The official recognition of his inventions is recorded in his
United States patents numbered 674,846, the application
for which was filed December 20, 1897, and 609,154, for
which the application was filed in 1898. A reproduction
of the first is printed in full in the appendix of this work.
The data and claims of the second are as follows :

*No. 609,154, Oliver J. Lodge, Liverpool, England, Dated August 16, 1898.
Application filed February 1, 1898.*

CLAIM 1. In a system of Hertzian-wave telegraphy, the combination,
with a pair of capacity areas, of a self-inductance coil inserted between them
electrically for the purpose of prolonging any electrical oscillations excited
in the system, and constituting such a system a radiator of definite frequency or pitch.

CLAIM 2. In a system of Hertzian-wave telegraphy, the combination,
with a pair of capacity areas, of a self-inductance coil inserted between them
electrically for the purpose of prolonging any electrical oscillations excited
in the system, thus constituting the system a resonator or absorber of definite frequency or pitch, and a distant radiator of corresponding period
capable of acting cumulatively.

CLAIM 3. In a system of Hertzian-wave telegraphy, the combination,
with a pair of capacity areas, of electrical means having a spark-gap inserted
between them and serving to syntonize them, and means for bridging or
shunting the spark-gap, whereby the apparatus is adaptable for use at will
either as a radiator or resonator.

CLAIM 4. In a system of Hertzian-wave telegraphy, the combination,
with a pair of capacity areas, of a number of self-inductance coils having

different amounts of self-induction, each of which is capable of being switched in or out of circuit, serving to syntonize any such radiator to a corresponding resonator or *vice versa*, whereby signaling may be effected between any two or more correspondingly-attuned stations without disturbing other differently-attuned stations.

CLAIM 5. In a system of Hertzian-wave telegraphy, the combination, with a pair of capacity areas, of a variably-acting self-inductance coil, serving to syntonize such a radiator or resonator to any other such resonator or radiator, whereby signaling may be effected between any two or more correspondingly-attuned stations without disturbing other differently-attuned stations.

CLAIM 6. In combination, a pair of capacity areas connected by a coil of wire serving as the radiator in a system of Hertzian-wave telegraphy, means for syntonizing such radiator, and means for charging it by aerial disruption or impulsive rush.

CLAIM 7. In a system of Hertzian-wave telegraphy, the combination of a pair of capacity areas such as h, h', means for syntonizing such capacity areas, a receiving-circuit completed through one or both of such capacity areas, and means for bridging over the discharge-gap between such capacity areas when they are to be used as a receiver, whereby such capacity areas are rendered adaptable for use at will either as a radiator or resonator.

CLAIM 8. In combination, in a system of syntonic Hertzian-wave telegraphy, a pair of capacity areas, a self-inductance coil and a secondary coil surrounding said self-inductance coil, which secondary coil forms part of the coherer-circuit substantially as and for the purpose set forth.

CLAIM 9. The combination, in the receiving-circuit of a system of Hertzian-wave telegraphy, of a variably-acting self-inductance coil, connecting the capacity areas, a coherer, a battery, a receiving instrument, and a shunt across the coils thereof substantially as and for the purpose set forth.

Declaration in Marconi's U. S. Patent. — Regarding priority in invention, a quotation from the specification of the reissue of Marconi's first American patent is herewith given. It may be explained that statements of this character embodied in a patent do not constitute official recognition, such recognition being confined to the allowed claims.[1]

[1] See pp. 102, 103, and 200.

"I am aware of the publication of Professor Lodge of 1894 at London, England, entitled 'The Work of Hertz,' and the description therein of various instruments in connection with manifestations of Hertz oscillations. I am also aware of the papers by Professor Popoff in the ' Proceedings of the Physical and Chemical Society of Russia' in 1895 or 1896; but in neither of these is there described a complete system or mechanism capable of artificially producing Hertz oscillations, and forming the same into and propagating them as definite signals, and reproducing, telegraphically, such definite signals; nor has any system been described, to my knowledge, in which a Hertz oscillator at a transmitting-station, and an imperfect-contact instrument at a receiving-station, are both arranged with one terminal to earth and the other elevated or insulated ; nor am I aware that prior to my invention any practical form of self-recovering imperfect-contact instrument has been described. I believe that I am the first to discover and use any practical means for effective telegraph transmission and intelligible reception of signals produced by artificially formed Hertz oscillations."

INITIAL AMERICAN PATENT OF GUGLIELMO MARCONI.

For United States Patent No. 586,193, the application by Marconi was filed December 7, 1896. The patent was issued July 13, 1897, with fifty-six claims, and remained as the record until June 4, 1901, when it was reissued as No. 11,913, in which the fifty-six claims were replaced by twenty-four. The complete reissued record is reproduced in the appendix of this work.

MARCONI'S UNITED STATES PATENTS.

Initial American Patent. — Considering now the reissued claims of the initial American patent of Marconi, the first one is a combination of the three elements, — an imperfect contact, a current through it, and a receiving instrument operated by the influence of distant oscillations on the contact. The second claim is also a combination of three elements, — an imperfect contact, a current through it, and means operated by the circuit to shake the imperfect contact.

CLAIM 3.   The third claim, while it combines as many as seven elements, appears to be an essential one.   It reads :

> A spark-producer,
> An earth-connection to one end of the spark-producer,
> An insulated conductor to the other end,
> An imperfect contact,
> An earth-connection to one end of the contact,
> An insulated contact to the other end,
> A circuit through the contact.

The important features of this combination, the use of ground connections with the transmitter and the receiver, is suggested by Dolbear's patent.   (See Appendix.)

Metal Shield Around Receiver.[1] — Marconi's second patent, by filing of application, is No. 624,516.   It has three claims of length, each bringing forward as one element a metallic box inclosing the receiver.   The object of this is to prevent injury to the receiver, on account of its close proximity to the sparking appliance when both sender and receiver are used at one station.   Metal screens to protect the receiver from a near-by transmitter are disclosed in Marconi's initial American patent filed in 1896.   The same principle is also the subject of Professor Lodge's third claim in No. 674,846, filed a year earlier than Marconi's 624,516, and is fully described in Lodge's specification.   Consequently a broad claim was not possible at the date of filing of the metal shield application.

Marconi's Third American Patent. — Marconi, on January 5, 1899, filed an application for a U. S. patent which

---

[1] See Figs. 69 and 70 in Part IV., with accompanying descriptions.

was issued June 27, 1899, as No. 627,650. Its first claim is here broken into paragraphs to distinguish the different elements.

CLAIM 1. In a receiver for electrical oscillations, the combination of
An imperfect contact (*the coherer*),
A local circuit through it,
An induction coil,
A capacity (*either a condenser or the earth*),
A conductor connected to one end of the primary of the coil (*the high wire*),
A connection between the other end and the capacity (i.e., *the primary to earth*),
Connections between the ends of the imperfect contact and the ends of the secondary coil,
A condenser in one of the latter connections.[1]

There are eight claims, all of them in connection with a receiver for electrical oscillations. Claim 2 adds to the combination in No. 1 as protection to the coherer, choking coils, which also appear in the initial Marconi American patent. Claims 3, 4, 5, and 6 introduce an induction coil in which the primary and secondary windings are each of but a single layer ; and claims 7 and 8 modify these layers in that they are composed of wires not exceeding one-fiftieth centimeter in diameter ($\frac{1}{125}$ inch). Regarding single-layer windings, Marconi himself in future patents made continued modification.

MARCONI'S FOURTH, FIFTH, AND SIXTH AMERICAN PATENTS.

On June 13, 1899, Marconi filed an application which was afterwards divided and finally issued in the form of three U. S. patents, numbered respectively 647,007,

[1] Italicized words in parentheses supplied by the author as explanatory.

647,008, and 647,009.   In these specifications is much matter in common, the forty claims for the three patents being
made thus voluminous to cover technical points.   Two
drawings have been selected, — Fig. 32, the main illustration of both the first and third of the series, and Fig. 33,

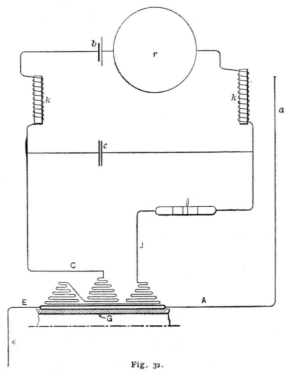

Fig. 32.

the principal drawing in the second of the series.   The
quotation here presented is common to all three of the
series :

"This invention relates to improvements in the apparatus described in
the specification of Patent No. 627,650, granted to me June 27, 1899.   In

that specification I described connecting the aerial conductor to a capacity
which may be the earth through the primary of an induction-coil, the ends
of the imperfect contact or sensitive tube being connected to the ends of the
secondary.   In place of winding both the primary and secondary in single
layers, as claimed in that specification, the coils are now either made very
short (not much exceeding two centimeters in length) or else are wound in
sections.   The number of turns in the successive layers of the secondary

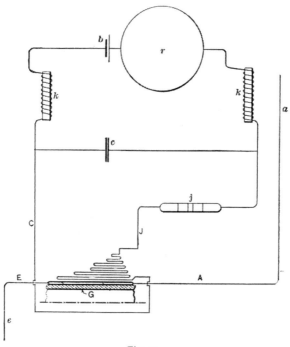

Fig. 33.

(and sometimes of the primary also) should diminish as the distance from
the center increases ; but this, although preferable, is not essential.   It is
also found desirable to connect direct to the sensitive tube or imperfect
contact (not through the condenser) the end of the secondary which is
farthest away from the nucleus or axial line of the coil.

    " In description of Figs. 32 and 33, *a* is the aerial conductor; *b*, a local
battery ; *c*, a condenser ; *e*, a connection to earth or other suitable capacity ;

j, a sensitive tube or imperfect contact; *k* are choking-coils, and *r* a relay working a signaling or other instrument. The diagrams of the coils are greatly enlarged half-longitudinal sections, but are not strictly to scale. In place also of showing the section of each coil or layer of wire as a longitudinal row of dots or small circles, as it would actually appear, it is for simplicity shown as a single continuous longitudinal straight line. A is the end of the primary, which is connected to the aerial conductor *a*, and E is the end connected to earth or a capacity. J is the end of the secondary, which is directly connected to the sensitive tube or imperfect contact *j*, and C is the end which is connected to it through the condenser. G is a glass tube on which the coils are wound. The wires are preferably insulated by a single covering of silk."

Claims 1, 2, and 16 fairly illustrate the inventive scope of the first one of this group, No. 647,007, and are as follows :

CLAIM 1. In a receiver for electrical oscillations, the combination of an imperfect electrical contact, a local circuit through it, an induction-coil, the secondary of which consists of several layers, the number of turns in the outer layers being less than in those next the primary, a capacity connected to one end of the primary, a conductor connected to the other end, and connections between the ends of the imperfect contact and the ends of the secondary.

CLAIM 2. In a receiver for electrical oscillations, the combination of an imperfect electrical contact, a local circuit through it, an induction-coil, the secondary of which consists of several layers, the number of turns in the outer layers being less than in those next the primary, a capacity connected to one end of the primary, a conductor connected to the other end, connections between the ends of the imperfect contact and the ends of the secondary, and a condenser in one of the latter connections.

. . . .

CLAIM 16. In a receiver for electrical oscillations, the combination of an imperfect electrical contact, a local circuit through it, an induction-coil, the primary of which consists of two wires connected in parallel, wound in *four* layers, the first and second layers being formed of one wire and the third and fourth of the other, the secondary of which consists of several layers, the number of turns in the outer layers being less than in those next the primary, and wound unsymmetrically with a lump at one end, a capacity connected to one end of the primary, a conductor connected to the other end, connections between the ends of the imperfect contact and the ends of the secondary, and a condenser in one of the latter connections.

. . . .

Claims 1, 2, and 4 of the *second of the group* are inserted to show the distinctive features of that patent. Words are Italicized by the author to mark a phrase which does not occur in the first patent, but is found in all three of the following claims :

CLAIM 1. In a receiver for electrical oscillations, the combination of an imperfect electrical contact, a local circuit through it, an induction-coil, the secondary of which consists of several layers, the number of turns in the outer layers being less than in those next the primary, a capacity connected to one end of the primary, a conductor connected to the other end, connections between the ends of the imperfect contact and the ends of the secondary, *and a condenser in the connection to the inner end of the secondary.*

CLAIM 2. In a receiver for electrical oscillations, the combination of an imperfect electrical contact, a local circuit through it, an induction-coil, the secondary of which consists of several layers, the number of turns in the outer layers being less than in those next the primary, and wound unsymmetrically with a lump at one end, a capacity connected to one end of the primary, a conductor connected to the other end, connections between the ends of the imperfect contact and the ends of the secondary, *and a condenser in the connection to the inner end of the secondary.*

CLAIM 4. In a receiver for electrical oscillations, the combination of an imperfect electrical contact, a local circuit through it, an induction-coil, the primary of which consists of two wires connected in parallel, wound in two layers, the secondary of which consists of several layers, the number of turns in the outer layers being less than in those next the primary, and wound unsymmetrically with a lump at one end, a capacity connected to one end of the primary, a conductor connected to the other end, connections between the ends of the imperfect contact and the ends of the secondary, *and a condenser in the connection to the inner end of the secondary.*

Of the last of the series but one claim, the sixteenth, is shown where the Italicized word " two " is its only distinction from claim 16 of the first of the series, in which the word " four " is also found in Italics.

CLAIM 16. In a receiver for electrical oscillations, the combination of an imperfect electrical contact, a local circuit through it, an induction-coil, the primary of which consists of two wires connected in parallel, wound in *two* layers, the secondary of which consists of several layers, the number of turns in the outer layers being less than in those next the primary, and wound unsymmetrically with a lump at one end, a capacity connected to one end of the primary, a conductor connected to the other end, connections between the ends of the imperfect contact and the ends of the secondary, and a condenser in one of the latter connections.

INVENTION OF IMPROVED TRANSMITTING KEYS, SEVENTH AND EIGHTH AMERICAN PATENTS OF MARCONI.

Patent No. 650,110, filed December 28, 1899, is a modification of No. 650,109, filed on October 12 of the same year. The diagram which illustrates the former is shown as Fig. 77 in connection with "Keys," Part IV. The difference between the two patents is that in the first a connection is made from that electrode of the spark-gap which connects with the high wire to an insulated back terminal on the sending-key of the transmitting operator; while in the second patent the high wire connecting directly with the insulated back terminal of the transmitting key does not make actual contact with the electrode of the spark-gap, but, instead, is brought very near to it.

The first claim of 650,109 is as follows :

CLAIM I. The combination of the primary and secondary of a sparking appliance, a battery and key in circuit with the primary, an aerial conductor connected to one terminal of the secondary, a receiver, means for connecting the said terminal to the receiver, and a capacity connected to the other terminal.

In the second claim there are substituted for the last eight words of Claim 1 the words "and an earth connection connected to the other terminal."

The first claim of No. 650,110 is as follows:

CLAIM 1. The combination of the primary and secondary of a sparking appliance, a battery and key in circuit with the primary, an aerial conductor led in close proximity to one terminal of the secondary, means for connecting the said aerial conductor to the receiving instrument, and a capacity connected to the other terminal.

The change of phrase noted in the companion patent, whereby "capacity" is substituted for "earth connection," occurs here also.

NINTH AMERICAN PATENT OF MARCONI.

In Fig. 34 there is shown a new set of connections in which the secondary winding of a step-down induction coil is divided into two parts, a condenser is placed between the two parts, and the relay circuit is connected to them on each side of that condenser. This diagram is the principal drawing of U. S. Patent No. 668,315, issued on February 19, 1901, the application for which, however, was filed July 17, 1900. While it is not the broadest claim, No. 4 offers the best brief to illustrate the invention. It is given here with interpolated explanatory references as follows:

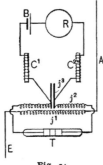

Fig. 34.

CLAIM 4. In a receiver for electrical oscillations, the combination of an induction coil, the secondary of which is wound in two parts (see j_2, Fig. 34), an aerial conductor connected to one end of the primary (A), a capacity connected to the other end of the primary (E), a detector or coherer connected to the outer ends of the secondary (T), a condenser across the inner ends of the secondary (j_3), a local circuit connected to the condenser (B R), choking coils between the local circuit and condenser (C1C2).

No. 1, the broadest claim, has but five elements, and reads as follows :

CLAIM 1. In a receiver for electrical oscillations, the combination of an induction-coil, the secondary of which is wound in two parts, an aerial conductor connected to one end of the primary, a capacity connected to the other end of the primary, a detector connected to the outer ends of the secondary, and a local circuit connected to the inner ends of the secondary.

The wording of one part of the specification leads to the belief that at the date of its filing, July 17, 1900, the inventor was beginning to question the efficacy of the

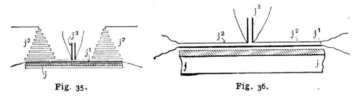

Fig. 35.   Fig. 36.

unsymmetrical winding advocated in former patents, although he still gives to it, as Fig. 35, precedence in order of description.   The arrangement shown in Fig. 36, however, is spoken of as one from which " very good results have been obtained."   In it each half of the secondary consists of one hundred and sixty turns in a *single* layer.   The specification states that in using coils in which the secondary winding consists of one layer, the inventor had noticed that the best results were had when the length of the secondary winding was approximately equal to the length of the aerial conductor employed at the transmitting station, an observation somewhat in line with Professor Slaby's assertion that there is a law of transmission which governs the length both of the emitter and the antenna.[1]

[1] See in connection with Slaby, p. 58.

DOUBLE WAVE—GATES.   TENTH AMERICAN PATENT OF
MARCONI.

At this writing the final Marconi patent, so far as
known, is No. 676,332.   The application was filed February 23, 1901, and it was issued on June 11 of the same
year.   It relates to the employment of double emitters

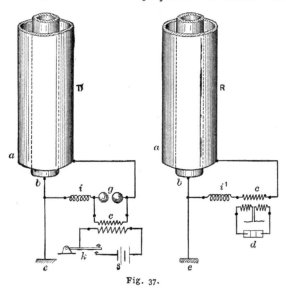

Fig. 37.

and antennae.   These double conductors are shown either
as concentric cylinders separated by an appreciable air-
space, or as two distinct vertical wires, or as an aerial
terminal consisting of two conductors arranged concentri-
cally, the inner one being a solid wire covered with an
insulating substance, and the outer being a tube fitting
closely around the insulation of that which forms the core.

The typical diagram is Fig. 37, in which it may be noted that the inner conductor has one branch to earth and one through an inductance and the spark-gap to the outer one. In other drawings the patentee shows at the transmitting station the wire connecting secondary coil c with inductance i to the left as having a pointed top, and resting against one of the coils of i, thus indicating that the inductance may be varied. The scope of this final Marconi patent may be shown by an analysis of its five claims as follows :

CLAIM 1. Element one, — Two aerial oscillation-producing conductors insulated from each other. Element two, — An inductance connected in series with such conductors. Element three, — A producer of electric oscillations (a Ruhmkorff coil, for instance). Element four, — A signaling instrument controlling the spark-producer (as a key in the primary circuit).[1]

CLAIM 2. There is added to the combination in claim 1 a fifth element, a connection from one of the emitters to the earth.

CLAIM 3. Element one of first claim is modified by the statement that the two aerial oscillation-producing conductors are insulated from each other.

CLAIM 4. Pertains to a receiving station and has four elements : One. Two antennae insulated from each other. Two. An inductance connected in series with the two antennae. Three. An imperfect electrical contact.

CLAIM 5. Adds to the combination in claim 4 a connection from one of the antennae to the earth.

There occurs in the specification of the patent now under consideration the remark that while " Lodge shows two large oscillation-producing conductors and an inductance device connected between them," yet he does not " use a plurality of aerial oscillation-producing conductors." [2]

[1] Parenthetical phrases supplied by author.
[2] See claims 6 and 8, Lodge's patent, No. 609,154, p. 101, Part II.

THE WIRELESS TRANSMISSION PATENTS OF TESLA.

A number of inventions by Mr. Nikola Tesla have been described at length in Part I. Their relation to the general patent situation is, however, so complex, and may prove so far reaching that anything like an exhaustive discussion of such of his numerous patents as bear upon the art, would occupy many times the space which can be allotted in this work. Anything less than an exhaustive discussion would not do the subject justice. It has, therefore, been thought best to reproduce in the appendix, without any comment whatever, the numbers, titles, dates of filing and representative claims, of such patents as may seem to give to the inventor a monopoly of any of the methods and devices necessary to the proper working of a wireless telegraph system.

UNITED STATES PATENTS OF PROFESSOR REGINALD
A. FESSENDEN.

On August 12, 1902, there were issued to Professor Fessenden thirteen United States patents, which are here considered in the order of their filing as applications.

Fessenden's Initial United States Patents. — The first two, filed December 15, 1899, and numbered 706,735 and 706,736, are companion patents, one concerning the methods and the other the devices of the same improvements. The first claim of the method patent reads:

CLAIM I. " As an improvement in the art of transmitting signals electrically by electromagnetic waves, the method herein described, which con-

sists in the generation of electromagnetic waves at one station and transforming the energy of the currents generated by such waves at the receiving-station into the energy of motion, that is without the necessary interposition of a secondary or auxiliary generator for the production of such
motion."

The auxiliary generator referred to as omitted is presumably the battery which in coherer organizations actuates the relay. It will be observed that, as represented in
Fig. 55, Part IV., there is no source of energy whatever
at the receiving station.

To a feature of this invention attention is called by
another claim, as follows:

CLAIM 6. "As an improvement in the art of transmitting electrical energy by electromagnetic waves, the method herein described, which consists
in prolonging the oscillations of an energy-radiating conductor by energy
from a source external to the radiating-conductor and tuned to the period
of the radiating-conductor."

The external source here is condenser 18 in a shunt circuit around the spark-gap as shown in Fig. 44, Part IV.

Another novel feature is set forth in the ninth claim,
and explained by Fig. 53, Part IV., and the accompanying
description.

CLAIM 9. "As an improvement in the art of transmitting electrical
energy, the method herein described, which consists in varying the conductivity of a secondary circuit at the receiving-station by motion produced
by currents generated by electromagnetic waves."

The Device Patent. — The device patent 707,636 has
the same drawings as 706,735. Its claims cover in general the means and combination of means which are used
in the methods specified and claimed in its mate.

Fessenden's Patent for Electro-Magnetic Sending Conductor. — No. 706,737 was filed May 29, 1901. Here No. 17 is a characteristic claim for a sending conductor.

CLAIM 17. "A sending-conductor for electromagnetic waves having low resistance, small self-induction and great capacity."

An illustration of the above is found in reference number 1 of Fig. 38.

Another feature is the receiver of claim 12, which is shown in Fig. 55, Part IV. The claim entire reads, —

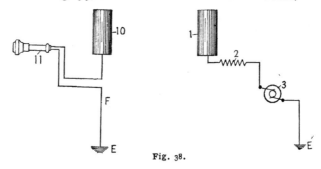

Fig. 38.

CLAIM 12. "A system for signaling by electromagnetic waves, having in combination a conductor adapted to radiate waves of low frequency, and a receiver dependent for its action upon a constant or independently-varying magnetic field and adapted to respond to currents produced by said waves."

Fig. 38, as a whole, illustrates a system covered fairly well by claim 21, which reads :

CLAIM 21. "A system for transmission of energy by electromagnetic waves, including in combination a radiating-conductor and a source of alter. nating electrical energy or potential, said radiating-conductor and source being co-ordinated and relatively adjusted to radiate a substantially continuous stream of electromagnetic waves of substantially uniform strength."

Fessenden's U. S. Patent for Localizing by the Use of a **Plurality of Tuned Circuits.** — The features of No. 706,-738, filed May 29, 1901, are well indicated by its claims 1 and 5 here quoted, and as an illustrating diagram reference is had to Fig. 26, Part I.

CLAIM 1. "In a system of signaling by electromagnetic waves, a receiving-conductor having a transforming device in series in the circuit, in combination with a circuit including a translating device, and having a local source of voltage and controlled by the transforming device and a source of voltage so arranged that its voltage will oppose the voltage from the local source operating the translating device.

CLAIM 5. In a system of signaling by electromagnetic waves, a sending-conductor adapted to maintain and to radiate persistent oscillations, in combination with a receiving-conductor and one or more secondary circuits controlled by the receiving-conductor, the ratio of inductance to capacity being larger in a secondary circuit than in the sending-conductor, a wave-responsive device included in a secondary circuit of a series, the several circuits being each tuned to correspond to the period of the sending-conductor."

Fessenden's United States Patent for Increasing the Capacity of the Wave-Gate. — The Fessenden patent 706,739 covers a device for surrounding the wave-gate with a medium of specific inductive capacity higher than air. Figs. 62 and 63 in Part IV. are respectively a plan and an elevation, and are there fully described. The first of the twenty claims may be quoted as follows :

CLAIM 1. "A conductor for radiating electromagnetic waves, in combination with a medium having an electrical constant on which the wave length depends of a value greater than that of air arranged in suitable relation to the conductor."

Fessenden's United States Patent for Localization by Generating and Receiving Two Sets of Waves of Different Periodicities. — No. 706,740, filed September 28, 1901, is an ingenious device for the localization of signals. It is described at length in connection with Fig. 28, Part I. Of the nine claims two are sufficient for illustration.[1]

CLAIM 1. "In a system of signaling by electromagnetic waves, the combination of a source of waves of different periodicities and two or more receivers responsive respectively to the differing waves or impulses, and a wave-responsive device operative when the waves or impulses attain a certain predetermined phase relation.

CLAIM 6. In a system of signaling by electromagnetic waves, the combination of means at the sending-station for generating two or more sets of waves of different periodicities, and a wave-responsive device at the receiving-station operative by the conjoint action of such set of waves."

Fessenden's Wireless Telephony.—The interesting claim of Patent No. 706,747, filed September 27, 1901, is the fourteenth referring to Wireless Telephony as follows :

CLAIM 14. " In a system for transmission of speech by electromagnetic waves, the combination at the sending-station of means for the practically continuous generation of electromagnetic waves, a telephone-transmitter for modifying the character of the waves or impulses, and a telephone-receiver at the receiving-station responsive to currents generated by the electromagnetic waves."

An illustration of the above is Fig. 27 in Part I., and there described.

Fessenden's High Pressure Spark-Gap. — Professor Fessenden's Patent 706,741, filed November 5, 1901, is for a device to maintain a certain definite relation between the resistance and the self-inductance and capacity of the sending mechanism, regardless of the potential employed. It is described at length in connection with Figs. 46 and 47, Part IV. To indicate its patentable scope, two of its claims are subjoined.

CLAIM 5. "An apparatus for the generation of radiation, having in combination a conductor for radiating electromagnetic waves, and sparking

[1] See in Part I. description of Tesla Patents, Nos. 723,188 and 725,605, and in Appendix their dates and claims.

terminals, all gaps between sparking terminals being occupied by insulating material under pressure greater than atmospheric pressure, substantially as set forth.

CLAIM 11. An apparatus for the generation of radiation having in combination a conductor for radiating electromagnetic waves and sparking terminals, all gaps between sparking terminals being occupied by insulating material under pressure above a certain critical high pressure."

Fessenden's Patent for a Selective System. — In connection with "Keys" in Part IV., will be found as Figs. 74, 75, and 76, a reproduction of the third sheet of drawings of the Fessenden Patent No. 706,742, filed June 6, 1902.

This document is long, containing five sheets of drawings, six printed pages of specifications, and twenty-nine claims.

To show its features, five of the claims follow:

CLAIM 5. "In a system for signaling, &c., by electromagnetic waves, the combination of a conductor adapted to radiate electromagnetic waves, means for causing the radiation of electromagnetic waves from said conductor, and means for modifying one or more of the characteristics of said waves.

CLAIM 9. In a system of signaling by electromagnetic waves, the combination of a conductor and a spark-gap with means for changing the function of the conductor, *i.e.*, from sending to receiving without bridging or disconnecting the spark-gap.

CLAIM 16. In a system of signaling by electromagnetic waves, the combination of a receiving-circuit, a series of receivers, and means shifting any desired one of said receivers into and out of operative relation to the receiving-conductor.

CLAIM 21. A system of signaling by electromagnetic waves, having in combination a sending-conductor and a key provided with fingers adapted to be brought into contact in succession with the sending-conductor at different points.

CLAIM 26. A system of signaling by electromagnetic waves, having in combination therewith means for indicating to a third station during sending or receiving that such sending or receiving station is busy."

Fessenden's Patent for Recording on Photographic Paper. — Patent No. 706,743, filed June 26, 1902, is for a method of catching the signals on photographic paper, and at the same time and in the same procedure applying chemicals to fix and develop them. There are but three claims, which are herewith reprinted.

CLAIM 1. "As an improvement in the art of signaling by electromagnetic waves, the method herein described, which consists in producing interpretable characters or symbols on a strip or film by chemical action produced by currents generated by electromagnetic waves.

CLAIM 2. As an improvement in the art of signaling by electromagnetic waves, the method herein described, which consists in affecting a sensitive strip or film by currents generated by electromagnetic waves.

CLAIM 3. As an improvement in the art of signaling by electromagnetic waves, the method herein described, which consists in producing interpretable characters or symbols on a strip or film by chemical action induced by electric currents generated by electromagnetic waves."

Fessenden's   Electromagnetic-Receiving-Device. — No. 706,744, filed July 1, 1902, is for an electromagnetic receiving-device. It is described at length in connection with Fig. 59, Part IV. The first three claims are sufficiently characteristic to show its patentable scope.

CLAIM 1. "A receiver for currents produced by electromagnetic waves consisting of a conductor having small heat capacity.

CLAIM 2. A receiver for currents produced by electromagnetic waves consisting of a conductor having small radiating-surface.

CLAIM 3. A receiver for currents produced by electromagnetic waves consisting of a conductor having low resistance and small heat capacity substantially as set forth."

Fessenden's Patent for System. — There will be found in connection with Fig. 29, Part I., a long description of the invention embodied in No. 706,745, filed July 1, 1902. The patent is for a system, and presumably presents the culmination of Mr. Fessenden's labors. Of its thirty claims the twenty-ninth may be quoted.

CLAIM 29. "A system of signaling by electromagnetic waves, having at the receiving-station a closed tuned secondary circuit and a constantly-receptive, current-operated, wave-responsive device, in combination with a source of persistent radiation at the sending-station."

Fessenden's Wave-Chute Patent. — Professor Fessenden's patent, No. 706,746, filed July 1, 1902, is for a wave-chute. It is fully described in connection with wave-gates, and illustrated by Figs. 64 and 65, Part IV. One claim is as follows.

CLAIM 5. "In a system for the transmission of energy by electromagnetic waves, a sending-conductor for radiating such waves, and an artificial ground connected to the lower end of the sending-conductor and connected at its outer end to ground."

NOTICEABLE GROUP OF INVENTORS.

It is impossible within the limits of this volume to mention, even briefly, all the inventions in this young art, for they are already numbered by hundreds. There is a noticeable group of inventors who assign, either directly or indirectly, to the American Wireless Telegraph Company. Among them Mr. A. F. Collins and Mr. Harry Shoemaker are prominent, the latter being especially prolific. Unfortunately there is no public record of quantitative results by which the merits of their inventions may be measured.

EHRET'S COMBINATION OF COHERER AND ANTI-COHERER.

The patent of Mr. Cornelius D. Ehret, already noticed at some length as of promise,[1] is deserving of consideration from an inventive standpoint. It is numbered 699,158. The application was filed December 3, 1901, and the issue is dated May 6, 1902. It contains twelve claims, all of value. Three of them are herewith reprinted.

CLAIM 1. "In a signaling system the combination of dissimilar wave-responsive devices conjointly controlling a translating device.

CLAIM 7. In a receiver the combination of a coherer and an anti-coherer conjointly controlling a translating device.

CLAIM 12. In a receiver the combination of a coherer and an anti-coherer, a local circuit controlled by each, a coil of a relay included in each circuit, said coils operating differentially on the magnetic circuit of each relay, substantially as described."

PUPIN PATENTS.

Dr. M. I. Pupin, of Columbia University, has taken out two United States patents for multiple telegraphy *with conductors*. His claims, however, may have so broad a scope as to cover the principle of selective signalling by means of electrical resonance ; and for this reason it is reported that his rights have been purchased by the Marconi interests. The numbers are respectively 707,007, and 707,008, and both were issued on August 12th, 1902. Application for the first was filed February 23rd, 1894. As an illustration of their bearing upon wireless telegraphy, claim number one of the earlier patent (707,007) is herewith quoted :

[1] See p. 84 and Fig. 30 in Part I.

"CLAIM I. The method of distributing electrical energy which consists in throwing upon a common conductor a number of alternate currents of different frequencies and distributing the several energies of these currents each selectively to a separate electrical device substantially as described."

SUMMARY.

There is in Part I an account of the transmission of electric signals by Morse in 1842 across a body of water; and a similar achievement by Lindsay some ten years later. In the next decade James Clark Maxwell published his interpretation of electrical phenomena as a propagation of ether waves, differing from light only in the lesser number of vibrations within a given unit of time. In 1882 Dolbear applied for a United States Patent for a method of telephonic transmission across space without wires; and in 1885 Edison applied for one to cover methods and devices similar to Dolbear's. It seems, however, that the true period of invention in the field of ethereal transmission extends from the discovery of the minute sparks in the bent wire at Carlsruhe in 1886, to the reception of the Poldhu signals at Cape Race in 1901; that the first transmission was due to Hertz, and the discovery of the properties of the filings to Calzecchi-Onesti; that the researches of Branly gave to the world the laws which govern the action of the coherer; that Lodge sealed the filings in a vacuum, applied to the coherer thus improved the principles of electrical resonance, and in a laboratory combined the various elements which make a wireless telegraph; that Tesla discovered many of the laws governing high frequencies and great pressures and devised means for the production and effective insulation of high potentials; and finally Marconi combined the results of these various discoverers in a system by which signals were observed at the distance of two thousand miles.

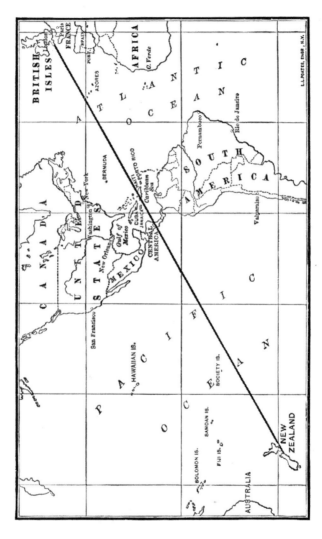

Fig. 39. — Marconi's projected line of communication. England to New Zealand.

PART III.

THE COMPARATIVE MERITS

OF WIRELESS TELEGRAPHY AND OF TELEGRAPHY BY WIRES AND CABLES—AND THE COMMERCIAL OUTLOOK FOR EACH.

THE history of the useful arts is evidence of the fact that each new development adapts itself to an especial field ; that old methods and devices, which seemed certain to be supplanted by new, often continue to be employed and even to multiply. The innumerable freight trains that now rumble between Buffalo and Albany have not displaced the mule and barge of Erie Canal ; and notwithstanding the existence of unnumbered freight-carrying iron steamers, wooden vessels with sail power are still being built on the Kennebec. Millions of electric lamps illumine the streets, theatres, hotels, and residences of New York City, yet "dollar gas" was very recently an issue in its politics. The pedestrians of our larger cities are compelled at each street crossing to calculate the relative speed of machine-moved vehicles ; yet the last United States Census records twenty-two millions of horses and mules ; and all the harness factories in the country at this writing are behind their orders. Telephone instruments are installed in every nook and corner of the City of New York, their daily connections counting into thousands ; yet the messenger business of the American District Telegraph has not decreased during the last seventeen years, and that company is still paying dividends.

It is the purpose of this section to speculate as to the influence that will be exerted by Wireless Telegraphy upon its predecessors and competitors in the field of distant communication. The new art has, of course, an exclusive and profitable employment in signaling from ship to ship on the ocean, and from ship to shore. The English Marconi Company already derives a revenue from tolls for communications between passengers on incoming steamships and the near shores, receiving about two hundred and fifty dollars a voyage from messages sent within a short distance of either side of the Atlantic. The Lloyds have adopted the system, and are requiring steamships that get the best insurance rates to be equipped with it. It is easy to prophesy that in the immediate future the telegraphic news of the world will be scattered like seed from the sower over the whole Atlantic and may be picked up by any vessel equipped with properly attuned apparatus ; but that it will render the present system of ocean cables obsolete is altogether improbable.

Ocean Cables as a Means of Communication. — The cables are an excellent medium for the transmission of signals ; they are in position ; and the money that has been expended to make and to place them cannot now be recovered. Neither bonded indebtedness, nor other form of financial obligation, will have any physical effect upon the efficiency of the cables as a means of communication.

Expression of the Cable Company's Official. — In this connection may be quoted an article from the *New York Sun* of March 4th, 1902, entitled " The Cable Company Cheerful " :

An expression of confidence in the ability of submarine cables to maintain their commercial supremacy in competition with wireless telegraphy was made yesterday by George G. Ward, Vice-President and General Manager of the Commercial Cable Company, in addressing as chairman the annual meeting of that company's shareholders in this city. Mr. Ward spoke as the representative of the officers of the company, who, he said, while they " did not intend to belittle the credit due to Mr. Marconi," for the advancement he has made in the field of wireless telegraphy, believed that submarine cables would hold their supremacy, even should wireless telegraphy " ever extend beyond its present experimental stage as regards trans-Atlantic or other long-distance transmissions." Mr. Ward added:

" Our shareholders must not overlook the fact that it has taken the Commercial Cable Company and its land line system some seventeen or eighteen years to perfect their organization for the distribution and collection of telegrams throughout the United States and the rest of the world. Assuming that the Marconi system should become perfected so that it could really compete in a commercial sense, and commercial requirements are very exacting, it is fair to say that it would take as many years to put the Marconi system in a position that would enable it to serve the public. Messages are now transmitted across the Atlantic and answers received in two and three minutes. A message experiencing a delay of ten or fifteen minutes means the defeat of the object of the sender. A most important point is the fact that 95 per cent of the Atlantic messages are expressed in code or cipher language, the words or ciphers having no connected meaning. The words or cipher groups frequently only differ from each other in single letters, yet they have widely different meanings, and an error in the transmission of one of their letters might have disastrous consequences. These are some of the commercial exactions or demands made upon the telegraphs. No one as yet even has pretended that the speed with which messages may be transmitted by wireless apparatus even approaches the speed of the aerial or submarine wire.

The company's net earnings for the year ended December 31, 1901, amounted to $2,259,897, a decrease of $19,770 compared with 1900. After payment of interest and dividends there was a balance of $409,538, against $493,003 in 1900."

Marconi's Belief. — Herewith is reprinted by permission from the *Century Magazine*, Marconi's own contention. This item was published about the same time as that of Vice-President Ward of the Cable Company :

"Mr. Marconi believes that his system may become a formidable competitor against the ocean cables. To compete on land is not so easy, as the lines there cost only one hundred dollars a mile, whereas the cables cost one thousand dollars a mile, and require expensive steamers to repair and maintain them. A transatlantic cable represents an initial outlay of at least three million dollars, besides the cost of its maintenance. A Marconi station can be built for sixty thousand dollars. Three of these, bringing the two worlds into contact, will cost only one hundred and eighty thousand dollars, while their maintenance should be insignificant. What his success will mean can be best grasped by considering the extent of the property which would be displaced thereby, although it is only since August 5th, 1858, that the first Atlantic cable was laid. There are now fourteen laid along the Atlantic bed, and in the whole world seventeen hundred and sixty-nine telegraph cables of various sizes, with a total length of almost one hundred and eighty-nine thousand nautical miles, enough to girdle the earth seven times. These require a great number of ocean-going cable steamers for their laying and repairs, and while the total value of the cables cannot be easily computed, it is known to be a fact that British capitalists have one hundred million dollars invested in cable stocks."

Marconi has said to his English stockholders that whereas the speed of the submarine cable is directly affected by length of transmission, the wireless system is not in the least affected by distance. That "it is just as easy to work at high speed across the Atlantic or Pacific as to work across the English Channel." He is confident of establishing direct communication between England and New Zealand.[1] He says that the curvature of the earth does not affect the signals, and that ultimately he will be able to send them all around the world.

Speed of Transmission over Ocean Cables. — Over the German Cable from New York to the Azores, two sets of

---

[1] See chart, Fig. 39, p. 124.

signals in opposite directions are simultaneously sent at a rate of about seventy words per minute for each circuit of a duplex transmission, making a total of one hundred and forty words.   This, it is said, is the best that is done over any long submarine conductor.   The principal limiting factor in this signaling is a delaying influence due to electrostatic capacity.   Professor Pupin of Columbia University, who has exhaustively investigated this subject, has pointed out that electrostatic capacity, being a storage of power, is an advantage rather than a detriment if properly controlled; and in pursuance of his plans for such control, it is reported that the Bell Telephone Company has equipped three circuits from New York to Chicago with "Pupin Coils," and that the results are an increase in the efficiency of speech-communication equivalent to one hundred per cent.

Professor Pupin is sanguine that equally good results will follow a similar treatment of ocean cables, but there is no way of demonstrating this fact in actual practice except by the construction of a new cable in conformity with his design.   He has been quoted in newspaper paragraphs as saying that the ultimate possibility in submarine telegraphy is a rate of one thousand words per minute ; and while it may be feasible to attain this speed it seems that conditions other than those connected with induction will require for such rapid work both a larger conductor and an increased mass of insulating material, thus entailing an expense in construction which may prove prohibitive ; and that a safer estimate of probable future speed is five hundred words per minute.

Progressive Invention in Cable Apparatus. — It may be said also that there is progressive invention in cable apparatus. Foresio Guarini, an Italian scientist of repute in the field of wireless telegraphy, has suggested the coherer as a device to be used in multiplexing ocean cables by means of electrical resonance. Chemical telegraphy, hereinafter explained, may also be mentioned in this connection. The foregoing suggestions will serve to point the fact that although etheric transmission has undoubtedly come to stay, the possibilities of wave propagation through copper still offer alluring fields of research.

WIRELESS TELEGRAPHY OVERLAND.

Hertzian-wave signaling overland, though still in embryo, will undoubtedly become an important factor. Marconi believes a thousand miles in one span to be a possible transmission. Guarini has been somewhat successful in devising automatic repeaters which may double or treble such a span. Fessenden predicts that a circuit will eventually be worked from New York to Chicago.

A difficulty in making the comparison between wave and wire signaling overland arises from the fact that the land telegraph systems with wires seem to be far behind their possibilities ; which is to say that the telegraph companies do not begin to do what they might ; and in order to present an intelligent view it is thought best to explain at some length the present situation of commercial telegraphy on land.

Controversy in the Electrical World. — There has recently occurred in the correspondence department of the *Electrical World* a controversy concerning the attitude of the Western Union Telegraph Company. This happening is fortunate in that the participants are representative men and have definitely announced their opinions. Professor Pupin had published a letter which virtually stated that the officials of the Western Union Telegraph Company were impervious to suggestions from inventors or scientists. The *Electrical World* editorially commenting upon this letter took the ground that the telegraph authorities, as compared with those in other electrical professions, had been noticeably backward in developing their art. The engineer of the Western Union Company replied that Professor Pupin's lack of practical experience in telegraphy probably accounted for his misapprehension.

The Morse System. — He also said that nothing had ever been found to equal what telegraphers call " Morse," a term used to define the method of reading signals by sound which renders it possible to write down a message as it is received, the telegram at the receiving end being ready for delivery as soon as the sending operator has finished his work. It was further said that in times of emergency and for some purposes the Wheatstone system had value.

Speed of Quadruplex. — The engineer of the Postal Telegraph Company gave some interesting data as to transmission by Quadruplex (a species of " Morse ") between New York and Boston, by which it appears that the average number of words sent over one wire by four operators is four thousand nine hundred and fifty per hour, or a little less than twenty-one words per minute per sender, or eighty-four words per minute per wire. It may be explained that in doing this work eight men are employed, four in sending and four in receiving.

A circuit between Boston and New York, however, does not furnish the most essential data, for it is but two hundred and fifty miles in length. The great telegraphic highways are the wires between New York and Chicago, which are a thousand miles long. Upon these circuits the quadruplex rate is likely to be nearer to sixty words per wire per minute ; but for the purposes of comparison we may use the data given at eighty words, as it is certain that this rate may not be exceeded.

The " Postal " engineer also stated that the public is not finding fault with the present telegraphic service, to which statement the reply may be made that the public is not fully enlightened. He further stated that the night or half-rate traffic " is naturally limited by reason of the splendid mail facilities between our principal cities."

Mail Service. — Following are actual facts in regard to mail service :

To transport a letter from a street box at 125th St. and 8th Avenue, New York City, to 39th Street and Cottage Grove Avenue in Chicago, requires forty-five hours ; consequently the securing of an answer to an inquiry by such means requires more than *four full days*.

A person in the business district of St. Louis desiring to send a letter to New York at two in the afternoon may just as well mail the letter at midnight. A letter registered on Thursday afternoon in St. Louis, with full postage, was not delivered in the business district of New York City until Monday morning.

First class mail matter deposited in the Post Office in

Detroit, Michigan, at six in the afternoon of Thursday, will not be delivered down town in New York until Saturday morning.

Between the service just described for two cents and the day rate of forty cents, and night rate of thirty cents for ten word telegrams, the telegraph companies have never been able to see an opportunity for employing at night their idle wires.

DIFFERENT TYPES OF TELEGRAPH APPARATUS.

Besides the "Morse," there is telegraphic apparatus known as the "Wheatstone," in which a paper ribbon is first perforated and then sent through a machine, recording at the distant end with ink marks upon paper tape ; the total speed of two sides of a "duplexed Wheatstone" is about two hundred words per wire per minute.

There is also the Buckingham page-printer, which first perforates a tape by means of a device like a typewriting machine, feeds the messages through a transmitting machine, and produces at the distant end typewritten copies at one hundred words per wire per minute.

Another device is the Murray page-printer, which practically accomplishes the same results as the Buckingham and attains about the same speed.

Another and recent device is the Rowland octoplex, by which eight circuits are worked over one wire, each circuit transmitting thirty words per minute, a total of two hundred and forty words per wire per minute. The sending is done by manipulating typewriters, typewritten copies being automatically produced at the receiving station.

It is said that the Wheatstone and Buckingham apparatuses are both regularly employed by the Western Union Telegraph Company, but the latter system was not mentioned by the company's engineer in the *Electrical World* controversy. If the Murray is in business use that fact is not known to the writer. The Rowland octoplex is said to be employed in Germany.

All of these machines are complex in detail and costly to construct. If there be considered, however, the total investment of money in a copper wire one thousand miles long and weighing perhaps four hundred pounds per mile, together with the cost of planting poles, of attachments to those poles, and the expense of patrol and maintenance, the claims of inventors of telegraphic machines that their apparatuses will pay for themselves in a short time seems well founded. Either the Buckingham or Murray page-printers, or the Rowland octoplex, are rated at a speed much greater than that of quadruplexed Morse. All of them save nearly fifty per cent in operating labor.

The officials, however, are obdurate, and while the equipment of perhaps one wire with a new device is occasionally allowed, the experiment seldom extends any further. The result of such policy in the past has produced a great array of abandoned machinery. After each trial, officials, engineers, and operating force are further strengthened in their admiration for the true and the tried ; and the disappointed inventors claim that to all arguments there is the same response, and to all appeals the same denial, — "There is nothing like Morse."

Morse Best Adapted to Certain Classes of Traffic. — No one denies that for the class of service that transmits orders from the New York Produce Exchange to the Chicago

Board of Trade it seems impossible to find a substitute for
Morse.   It is said that to the telegraphers in the Chicago
Trade Room even a typewriting machine is less facile than
the pen.   They write upon a blank, using copying ink;
when the message has been written, a moist piece of paper
is laid over the blank, the two are then fed between the
rubber rollers of a wringer, and there is quickly in hand
the original message, which may be handed the consignee,
and an impression copy for the company's files.

There are classes of business which require the same
rapidity of delivery as do those of the grain and stock
brokers, and for which Morse seems best adapted.   There
is, however, a traffic that comes from the general public
which is poorly handled.   It is not so much the way this
class of business is being transmitted with present facilities
as a matter of what might be done with other and better
devices and with the lower tariffs those devices would
warrant.

The charges for sending miscellaneous telegrams are the
same as for those of the preferred class.   Under favorable
conditions the telegraph companies may transmit an unpre-
ferred message fairly well; but if there be rain or wind or
excitement in Wall Street, or an election, or a political con-
vention, the wires are crowded; and having thus to contend
against frequent delays and high tariffs it is no wonder
that the number of these unfavored communications is
comparatively small.   As Mr. Delany, in one of the letters
of the recent discussion, has pointed out, there is no elasticity, no reserve power in the present telegraph service.
For the class of business just described, low rates and the
adoption of some of the new possibilities in multiplex or in
chemical telegraphy would undoubtedly increase the re-

ceipts of the telegraph companies and prove as well a boon to the public.

Chemical Telegraphy. — Almost coeval with Professor Morse's inventions are those of Alexander Bain, who declared as long ago as 1845 that by the chemical method he could transmit two thousand words per minute. A system based on this principle was tried by the Atlantic and Pacific Telegraph Company in 1875. Its officials made two mistakes, first ordering that it be used for all kinds of traffic, and then that its use be entirely discontinued. In the eighties the American Rapid Company tried the system again, but that company was unsuccessfully financed and soon collapsed.

The essential principle of chemical telegraphy is the fact that an impression is made whenever a current of electricity passes from a metallic point resting upon chemically treated moist paper to a conductor which connects with a part of the same circuit from another point on the paper. The action is electrolytic. A copper point leaves a red mark, an iron one a deep blue. The number of signals is governed by the volume of current, by the time of exposure, and to some extent by the electrostatic capacity of the conductor connecting the sending and receiving stations. It may be expressed by the equation

$$N = \frac{ET}{RK}$$

where N is the number of signals per unit of time, E the electromotive force, T time, R resistance, and K capacity.

While the author is not exactly informed as to quantitative results, it is safe to say that one five-thousandth of an ampere flowing from an iron point and impressed upon the sensitized paper for one second of time will leave a distinct mark ; and, conversely, that one-twentieth ampere unimpeded by capacity is sufficient current to produce two thousand words per minute, each word requiring from ten to twenty marks.

Description of Chemical Telegraph Apparatus. — Fig. 40 is a diagrammatic view of a chemical telegraph circuit, P being a source of current supply with one polarity, and N a second source, having a polarity the reverse of the first. B and B′ are brushes terminating respectively conductors

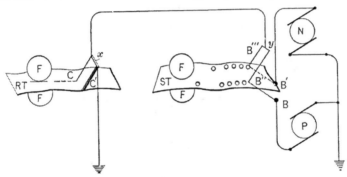

Fig. 40.

from P and N. B″ and B″ ′ are brushes on the surface of the sending tape ST which are brought into contact with B and B′ by reason of the holes in the paper being moved past them whenever the paper is pulled along by friction rollers FF. The yoke y is of conducting material, and consequently B″ and B″ ′ are electrically one piece which is connected to the line. At the far station RT is the chemically treated receiving tape, and resting upon it is an iron pen C which is joined by insulating material x to the platinum faced strip C′ called the spacing pen.

Operation of Chemical Telegraph. — Whenever a contact is made between brush B and the line by reason of the passing of one of the lower holes in tape ST, current flows across RT from C to C′ and colors the paper. After brush B has passed a hole, the charge of electricity which has become stored in the line flows to earth, and this secondary flow of current tends to prolong the mark. Thus the horizontal distance between a lower and an upper perforation impresses upon the sensitized paper either a long or a short mark according as the distance between any lower opening and its relative upper opening is long or short ; for whenever brush B′ is presented to line, it neutralizes the current flowing from C to C′, and the pen C ceases to color the paper.

Neutralizing Electrostatic Effects. — The system of positive and negative presentations is an improvement upon the earlier methods, which used current of one polarity only. Under the plan just illustrated, inductive influence is partly neutralized ; and by another and very simple contrivance in connection with the apparatus, the details of which the author is not at liberty to make public, electrostatic capacity seems to be under absolute control.

Speed. — The speed of the chemical telegraph is marvelous. Mr. Delany, the chief exponent of that kind of transmission, has succeeded in recording in a laboratory, and over an artificial line the equivalent of an ordinary telegraphic circuit one hundred and twenty-five miles in length, eight thousand words per minute. The author has seen an initial force of one hundred and ten volts transmit one thousand words per minute over an artificial line having the resistance and electrostatic capacity of a circuit between New York and Chicago. There is no reason why machines should not be devised by which two thousand words per minute may be sent with one hundred volts; nor is there any insuperable obstacle to the use of five hundred volts. Indeed the sending ten thousand words per minute over a copper wire a thousand miles long weighing four hundred pounds per mile is a possibility of the present development. Chemical transmission is now used by the Pennsylvania Railroad Company between Philadelphia and Altoona, and over the circuit employed, Mr. Delany has made a record of thirteen hundred words per minute. The line measures in resistance about fourteen hundred ohms, and is partly of iron wire.

There has been a plan for perforating paper tape by the manipulation of a Morse Key; and, as the action of a telegraph key is simply a down-and-up motion of a pivoted lever, this action may be reproduced at a considerable distance from the location of the sending operator. At the distant point the tape may be fed into a transmitter, and it may be reproduced by chemical signals over a second circuit.

To illustrate the plan of operation, a telegram from Newark, New Jersey, for delivery at Milwaukee, Wisconsin, under present conditions would be sent by Morse from Newark to the main office in New York City, thence by quadruplex to Chicago, thence by Morse to Milwaukee. By the perforator and chemical telegraph the Newark operator could make in the main office at New York a tape which would be used to transmit the message from New York to Chicago, where it would appear in the form of Morse signals on a moist paper ribbon, and this might

REESE LIBRARY
OF THE
UNIVERSITY
OF
CALIFORNIA

be handed to an operator in Chicago to be sent to Milwaukee by Morse.

In the first method the number of sets of human heads and hands occupied with the message is six; in the latter three, and consequently this latter presents just one-half the chance for errors. Moreover, in the actual time of passage the gain is considerable. The saving in plant, allowing to the second method five thousand words per minute, is as sixty to one over quadruplexed Morse; and would be as forty to one over any of the type-printers.

So much space has been given to the chemical system because of its development. It is wonderful that an organization so complete could have been perfected without the experience that comes from daily use; and more wonderful still, that having been thus perfected, it should be entirely neglected by the telegraph companies.

Other Means of Rapid Signaling. — There are undeveloped means of signaling, however, which to experts in wireless telegraphy seem certain of future attainment. Both Marconi and Fessenden are looking forward to machine transmission at a speed of five hundred words per minute, and they are also hopeful of multiplexing wireless circuits. Many of the obstacles, however, which loom up in the future of wireless telegraphy do not present themselves in transmission by wire, and there is every reason to suppose that a wire may not only be multiplexed many times, but that each of the phantom circuits, as they are called, may be made by machinery to convey some hundreds of words per minute; always with more certainty and speed than without the wires.

It is the apparent neglect of such great forces for which

the telegraph officials are held accountable by those acquainted with the facts.   Complication may not be urged,
because the chemical system, for example, is far simpler,
both in construction and operation, than is either the
duplex or the quadruplex or the typewriter devices.   The
passage over a single wire of thousands of words per minute is as well assured as is wireless telegraphy ; and if
brought into regular commercial use it may prove a
greater public benefit.   At present there is no outlook that
etheric signaling overland will ever attain to the tremen-
dous possibilities of telegraphy with wires.

Fig. 41. — City of St. Johns, Newfoundland, where the first transatlantic signal by space telegraphy was received from England.

PART IV.

APPARATUS.

NOMENCLATURE.

THE art which forms the subject-matter of this work is young and its nomenclature limited. " Wireless Telegraphy" itself but a negative term is temporarily supplying the need of a positive designation. Neither " radio-telegraphy" nor "wave-telegraphy" nor "etheric-transmission" satisfies. " Hertzian-wave telegraphy " is of unwieldy length and lacks euphony.

No single word suitably denotes every kind of instrumentality. affected by Hertzian or magnetic waves. "Detector" has been used in another sense. Mr. Tesla speaks of "sensitive-devices"; Mr. Fessenden and others of a "wave-responsive-device." " Responder " is too closely identified with the DeForest system to be acceptable to competitors. "Resonator," to denote a receiving device, is objectionable on account of its alliterative and structural similarity with "radiator," a transmitter.

Antenna is an excellent name for the conducting terminal that ends in air whenever the allusion is to a receiver of waves; but it is not sufficiently aggressive to express the opposite meaning. Emitter seems a good term for designating anything that serves to send impulses outward. The terminating conductor, however, being employed both as antenna and emitter, the necessity appears for that which denotes both uses. Mr. Fessenden speaks of an aggregation of five wires as a "harp." When the conditions are applicable, "high wire" is a good term, but not when cylinders or cones are used. The writer suggests as a comprehensive title, one used in this work, "wave-gate."

For the instrument that acts by diverse resistances of a sensitive device and thus translates the signals to a local

Fig. 42. — Elevating the kite-supporting wave-gate at Signal Hill, St. Johns, Newfoundland, December 12, 1901. — X Marconi.

and more powerful circuit, no better name than "relay" can be found : but to speak in that connection, of a "receiver," is to confuse it with the sensitive device itself.

The circuit which contains a radio-receiver battery and relay has occasionally been designated "local," not intrinsically a good term, and the less acceptable because to telegraphers it implies a second organization in contradistinction to the connections of the main line.

As suggested by Mr. Tesla's "sensitive-device," the train of apparatus having the radio-receiver for one element might properly be denoted the "sensitive circuit," and the battery which actuates the relay in that circuit the "closing battery."

For the wires and apparatus in series with the relay points, "recording-circuit," and for the energizing element of that group, "recording battery," are designations that should be clearly understood.

The terms "spark-producer," "oscillator," and "oscillation-producer" are synonymously applied to all apparatus that sends electric charges across the spark-gap.

"Induction-coil," the "primary" and "secondary" which compose it, and the "key" used to bring into operation the sparker, are terms well fixed in the public mind. The contact which rapidly opens and closes in the primary circuit is happily described in Marconi's patents as the "trembler-break."

As both Professor Lodge and Signor Marconi, partly for the purpose of broadening their patent claims, have insisted that both the earth and the wave-gate are "capacities," that term may not now be understood as confined in meaning to a condenser or to a Leyden jar.

TRANSMITTERS.

Ruhmkorff Coil. — Before the advent of wireless telegraphy the Ruhmhorff Coil was the standard spark-producer. Referring to Fig. 43 as an illustration of that coil, it may be described as follows:

In a position of rest the contact of spring T is in touch with that of upright K. By the closure of the break at switch S, battery B energizes circuit B–S–T–K, causing

the iron coil I to become magnetic. The iron face of
spring T is attracted towards coil I, but as the movement
forward immediately breaks contact at *a*, I is demagne-
tized, and the spring T resuming its first position in contact with K, coil I again becomes magnetized.   On
account of the quickly changing conditions in coil I, there
occur continuous and rapid vibrations at point *a*.

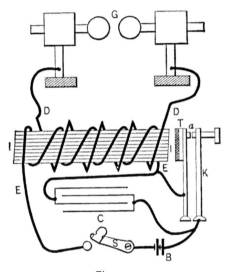

Fig. 43.

When, however, the current, after being made, is interrupted at point *a*, there takes place an electric discharge
which is, in effect, a flow of current in an opposite direction to the charge which has just been made.   This
reverse current, though of high pressure, is attenuated,
and has much less magnetic effect on the coil than the
initial one.   It tends, however, slightly to magnetize coil
I at a time when that coil should be non-attractive : and it

is also true that the high pressure generated is apt to burn the contacts at *a*.

The function of condenser C is to give back its charge with the same energy as that which emanates from the primary coil, thus neutralizing the bad effect of the primary coil's discharge. It is seldom, however, that the adjustments of the two forces are quite in balance, and consequently there is generally more or less imperfect action at *a*.

Marconi's Spark-Producer. — In Marconi's patent 11,913 is described a device which partially obviates the difficulty of corrosive points, in that, by means of a small electric motor, it causes one of the points of the vibrating break continuously to revolve. The spark in this patent is shown with an interposition of two balls in the center in an ebonite casing. The distance between the center balls is one twenty-fifth inch, and the inside distance between each of the terminating electrodes and the center balls one and one-half inches. The space between the two middle spheres is filled with vaseline oil. It is said that Mr. Marconi afterward discarded the c e n t e r globes and used a clear space between electrodes.

A Fessenden Transmitter. — F i g. 44 shows a transmitter de-signed by Mr.

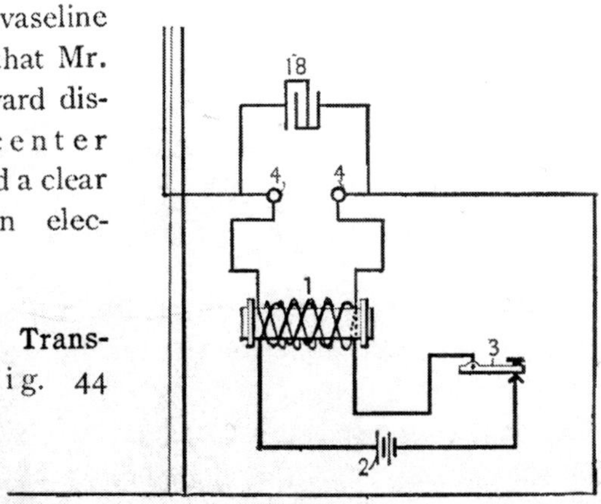

Fig. 44.

Fessenden, the patent for which was filed December 15, 1899. A distinctive feature is the condenser 18 bridging the spark gap between electrodes 4 – 4. This arrangement, the inventor says, is "for the purpose of maintaining sustained radiation," for "this shunt circuit by reason of its capacity stores up an additional amount of energy, and when a spark passes across the gap, since the sending conductor can radiate energy at a given rate, it must continue to radiate for a long time in order to dissipate this additional stored up energy."

A similar organization is shown in the Marconi patent 676,332, of later date than the Fessenden.[1]

Alternating Current Dynamo Instead of Interrupter. — The interrupter in the primary coil of a direct current sparking appliance being difficult of control with currents of high potential, it is the practice in large installations to employ steam power connected with an alternating current dynamo, the voltage of which may be "stepped up" by transformers ; and where steam power is not available, but energy is had from storage batteries, as in field operations, direct current from the batteries may be made to turn an electric motor by which an alternating current dynamo may be kept in motion to furnish the primary coil with energy to supply the spark gap.

Fessenden Dynamo as Direct Emitter. — The use of a dynamo for a direct emitter without the spark gap is shown in Fessenden's patent 706,737. He claims that he is able at once to produce a continuous train of radiant waves of substantially uniform strength, as distinguished from

[1] See Fig. 37 in Part II.

the well-known systems wherein the spark-discharge starts a train of waves of rapidly diminishing power, followed by relatively long intervals of no radia-tion. Fig. 45 is a diagram from the Fessenden patent where 1 is a short emitting wave-gate with large radia-ting surface, 2 a tuning inductance, 3 an alternating current dynamo with an earth connection.

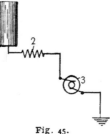

Fig. 45.

DeForest Transmitter. —The tran-smitter of the DeForest system uses an alternating cur-rent dynamo, a step-up transformer to increase the vol-tage; and discharges across a gap in which is interposed a detached conductor. The discharging electrodes and the interposed member are of the same shape and size, being disks of metal about one-quarter inch thick, and upon the sides or faces about one and one-quarter inches in diameter. The spark gaps upon each side of the middle disk measure about one sixty-fourth inch.

The DeForest experts claim that with electrodes of a surface relatively large as to the gap they get a "fat" spark, and that such a spark produces better results at the distant or responding end than would one of greater inten-sity but less volume.

A Fessenden Transmitter. — Figs. 46 and 47 are repro-ductions from drawings in one of Mr. Fessenden's patents, No. 706,641, filed November 5, 1901. The diagram of curves, Fig. 46, is a graphic representation of comparative efficiencies. The dots on horizontal line *c* indicate spark potential in inches, the vertical line *d* radiation or effective

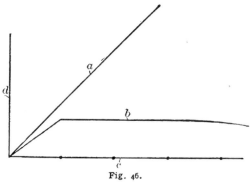

Fig. 46.

result. *b* is an efficiency curve which shows results obtained under usual conditions, viz.: that within a certain length of spark, about one inch, the resultant radiation of electromagnetic waves is approximately proportional to the length of spark; but that to increase the length of spark beyond one inch will result in no practical increase in radiation. The line *a* is another efficiency curve which is employed to demonstrate that with Mr. Fessenden's device, the wave force *d* is exactly proportional to spark gap *c* at whatever length the latter may be prolonged.

Referring to Fig. 47, 10 is a rod pointed at its lower end, surrounded by an insulating sleeve 11, and so introduced into the chamber 7 to form one electrode of the spark gap. The

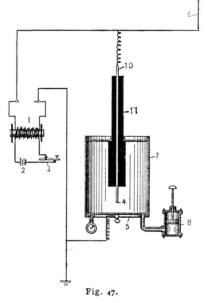

Fig. 47.

other electrode is the bottom plate of chamber 7, and thus one of the discharging terminals is a point 4, and the other a disk, 5. By means of pump 8, the air in chamber 7 is increased in pressure. It is found that when a certain critical pressure is reached, which, for instance, may be eighty pounds per square inch, the radiation for any length of spark becomes strictly proportional to the applied force.

The term "radiation" in the foregoing explanation, and as shown by the height of vertical line d of the curve diagram, is an expression of an applied energy, that, if doubled or trebled, doubles or trebles the distance from such energy for which a wave-responsive device may be made to indicate signals.

Considering as a generic term either "sensitive-device," or "wave-responsive-device," or "radio-receiver," or "detector," there may be made as classifications of it "coherers," "anti-coherers," "micro-radiophones," and "magnetic-radio-receivers."

Coherers. — If used without a qualifying word or prefix the word coherer is now understood to indicate that form of radio-receiver, which, being normally a high resistance, is, under the influence of Hertzian-waves, changed to a low resistance, becoming relatively a conductor, and remaining electrically conductive after the subsidence of the wave effect unless restored to its original state of resistivity by some sort of mechanical impact.

Filings Tube of Calzecchi-Onesti.   Decoherence by Revolving. — So long ago as 1886, Professor Calzecchi-Onesti placed copper filings between two brass plates and changed the electrical property of the filings from a state of high resistance to one of low resistance by passing through them the secondary impulse that occurs when an electric circuit is broken.   Afterward to facilitate decoherence he inclosed the filings in a revoluble glass tube.

Branly's Filings.   Tube Decoherence by Tapping. — Branly, 1891, discovered that the filings could be rendered conductive by the passage of electric sparks across an air-gap in their vicinity, and that they could be decohered by a slight jar.

Lodge and Fitzgerald Needle and Tin-Foil. — Dr. Lodge, in conjunction with Mr. Fitzgerald, made a coherer by causing the point of a sewing-needle to rest upon a strip of tin-foil. Later, this device was elaborated by contacting the needle point with a flat spring which was fixed within a clamp, the degree of pressure between point and spring being regulated by adjusting screws.

Branly's Tripod of 1902. — Professor Branly in 1902 placed a tripod having sharp steel points slightly oxidized upon a polished plane steel plate. A current of electricity passing from tripod to plate is, under normal conditions, subjected to a high resistance. This resistance is greatly diminished by Hertzian-wave effect, and may be re-established by so arranging a recording instrument, that immediately after the wave effect is discontinued, it will jar the plate.

Tesla's Filings Tube. Decoherence by Inversion. — In his patent No. 613,819, Mr. Tesla describes quite minutely a form of filings coherer which is decohered by being turned end for end, its position of rest being vertical. He makes the particles as nearly as possible alike in size, weight, and shape, having special tools to fashion them; and then oxidizes them uniformly by placing the grains for a given time in an acid solution of predetermined strength. He prefers not to rarefy the atmosphere within the tube, since by rarefaction it is rendered less constant in dielectric property. He recommends an air-tight inclosure and a rigorous absence of moisture. In another patent he specifies decoherence by continuous revolution, instead of by inversion, of the glass tube.

The " Silver " Coherer. — So far as is known by records of practical tests the most sensitive type of the class under consideration is the " silver " coherer. It is carefully described in the American reissue patent No. 11,913 of Marconi. Briefly the tube is one and one-half inches in length, and one-twelfth inch internal diameter. Within it are tightly plugged two pieces of silver wire, each one-fifth inch long. The space between these plugs at center is one-thirtieth inch. This minute space contains a powder composed of ninety per cent of nickel filings, and ten per cent of silver filings. The grains are as large as may be produced with a coarse file, and are coated with an almost imperceptible globule of mercury. The tube must be sealed. A perfect vacuum is not essential, but is desirable, and one of one-thousandth atmosphere has been used. Sensitiveness to waves may be increased by using a greater percentage of silver grains in the powder, or by decreasing the distance between the silver stops.

ANTI—COHERERS.

Fig. 48.

Hertz Detector. — The first radio-receiver in which cause and effect were observed and recognized was devised by Hertz in 1886. It consisted of a piece of wire, Fig. 48, bent into circular form, a small disconnecting gap being left in its circumference. If this device were suspended at some distance from a sparking Ruhmkorff Coil, there being no tangible connection between the coil and the circlet of wire, minute sparks could be seen to fly across the air-gap in the wire.

Righi Detector. — Professor Righi obtained similar action by holding at a few feet from a spark-producer a sheet of glass covered with tin-foil, the metal being separated by a fine diamond point into several longitudinal bands. Action at the electrodes of the induction coil resulted in sparking from band to band over the gaps in the tin-foil.

In 1899 a German scientist discovered that by placing a drop of water upon the slit formed by the tin-foil edges of the Righi bands, a very sensitive wave-detector was produced.

It is said the organizations just described differ from a coherer, in that the action of waves causes their electrical resistance to increase, an effect exactly opposite to that set up in the coherer proper. They are, therefore, named "anti-coherers," and differing in principle, are declared not to be subordinate to any patent claims which may cover a coherer method. There is a report, however, that the Marconi Company, presumably on the ground that the alleged anti-coherer is an "imperfect contact," is preparing to bring action for infringement against a competitor using an anti-coherer.

DeForest Responder. — The DeForest "responder" is the most prominent type of anti-coherer. Fig. 49 illustrates the receiving apparatus in which A and A′ are two small brass rods, or wires, connected respectively to the wave-gate and to the earth. D and D are hard rubber tubes, into which is fitted the glass tube C. F and F′ indicate the position of adjusting screws which serve to make greater or less the width of the gap which occurs at G between electrodes A and A′. B is a battery, generally of two or three dry cells, and T is a telephone. The

ends of the wires A and A′ are smeared at the gap G with
a minute quantity of a paste which the inventor has named
"goo." By means of the adjusting screws F F′ the ends
of A A′ are first brought together within the tube, and

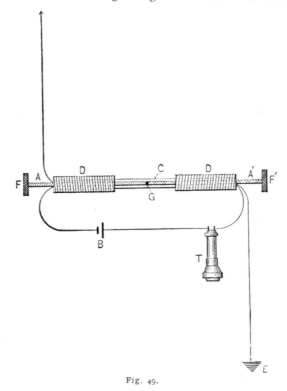

Fig. 49.

then slowly separated, until by repeated trials the amount
of space which is best for clear signals has been attained.

It will be understood that the "goo" thus bridges the
gap between the electrodes. Through a microscope the
paste is seen to lie in tiny globules which just touch one

another, but under the action of impinging waves these globules decompose and decohere, the effect being to increase the electrical resistance of the closed circuit, which, as in Fig. 49, contains a battery, a paste-filled gap G, and a telephone receiver.

Now a telephone receiver gives forth audible sounds in response to the slightest change in resistance, whether diminished or augmented; and thus, whenever a long-wave effect or a short-wave effect is produced at the sending end, it is indicated at the receiving end by long or short buzzing sounds in a telephone held or attached to the ear of an operator.

Ehret System. — Reference to the text and diagrams which describe the system of Mr. Ehret [1] will serve to explain one use of an anti-coherer in connection with a relay.

MICRO—RADIOPHONES.

Carbon Powder Wave-Detector of 1897. — There is record of the employment, about 1897, of a carbon powder coherer by which Professor Jervis Smith of Oxford University, England, maintained communication over more than a mile of space. So far as I can discover, this is the earliest specimen of a type that is now known as the micro-radiophone or micro-radio-receiver.

Popoff's Micro-Radiophone of 1900. — In May, 1900, Professor Popoff of Russia, as the result of experimentation, concluded that it was possible to eliminate the

[1] See Fig. 30, Part I., and accompanying description.

coherer and relay by substituting for both either a microphonic arrangement of steel needles, having their extremities resting upon plates of carbon, or by mixing steel
filings and carbon powder.

Shoemaker's Steel and Carbon Wave-Detector. — The
steel and carbon powder type of Professor Popoff has been
the subject of many patented inventions, one of which, by
Mr. Shoemaker of Philadelphia, consists of a number of
steel balls in a horizontal line, the space between the balls
being filled with carbon powder.

**Shoemaker and Pickard Needle and Carbon Wave-
Detector.** — Another invention was patented in the United
States, in August, 1902, by Messrs. Shoemaker and
Pickard. As expressed in the patent, —

" It comprises a wave-responsive-device whose essential elements are of
carbon and steel, respectively. A wave-responsive-device composed of

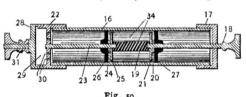

Fig. 50.

these materials has
the property of great
delicacy and sensi-
tiveness in respond-
ing to electrical ra-
diations, and has
also the desirable
property of regaining
its normal condition after the cessation of influence of electrical waves.

" More specifically, our invention comprises carbon terminal blocks, in
contact with which are steel or iron needles, which serve to close the
circuit from one carbon block to the other. As an alternative, however, it
is to be understood that the terminal blocks may be of steel, and that carbon filaments or rods may contact with them to close the circuit.

" The wave-responsive-device herein described is connected with any of
the wireless signaling systems in the same relation as the numerous types
of wave-responsive-devices heretofore used."

In Fig. 50, 16 is a glass tube or any suitable envelope, on the right-hand end of which is a metallic cap 17, through which is tapped the screw 18, which at its left-hand end screws into the central insulating portion 19, thereby clamping between said portion 19 and a brass nut 20 the carbon disk 21.

22 is a metallic cap upon the left-hand end of the tube 16, and from which extends into the tube rod 23, secured in said cap 22, and also into insulating block 19, thereby clamping between said block 19 and a nut 24 the carbon disk 25.

26 and 27 are disks of insulating material, which serve to center and steady the device in tube 16. It is to be noticed that the disks of carbon 21 and 25 are slightly smaller in diameter than the tube 16 for the purpose of preventing their contact with said tube during assemblage, inasmuch as such contact might serve to destroy the disks, due to the fact that they are thin and fragile. On to the left end of the cap 22 screws a cylindrical piece 28, forming between 28 and 22 a cavity 29,

Fig. 51.

designed to receive calcium chlorid or other desiccating material for keeping the air or other gas within the tube 16 perfectly dry. Communication between 29 and the interior of tube 16 is obtained by numerous holes, as 30. On the piece 28 is the binding-post 31, serving as one terminal of the device, while cap 17 or screw 18 serves as the other terminal.

Fig. 52.

Fig. 51 represents a plan view of one of the carbon disks — as, for example, 25 — which shows symmetrically-arranged small holes 32, while the inner large hole 33 permits the passage of the rods 18 or 23.

In Fig. 52 are shown the two carbon disks 21 and 25, supporting between them the needles 34.

This Shoemaker and Pickard organization is an elaboration of the Popoff microphonic receiver of 1900, and is typical of its class.

Fessenden.   Silver Ring and Knife-edge Contact. — Fig. 53 illustrates a radio-receiver designed by the United States Government expert, Mr. Fessenden. 7 represents a coil of wire which is a magnetic field for an armature 8, the latter being made preferably in the form of a

silver ring.   Ring 8 is balanced upon two knife edges 13
and 13', one of which, as 13, is formed of a good electrical
conductor, for example, silver ; and the other, 13', is out of
circuit.   A carbon block 14 is so arranged that the portion between it and knife edge 13 of the ring 8 forms part
of an electrical circuit.   Waves passing from the gate 6 to
the earth and energizing field coil 7 will cause the ring 8
to press upon the carbon block 14, thereby increasing the
conductivity of the contact between 8 and 14.

" When using a telephone-receiver as a recording instrument, the generator 15 is preferably of a character capable
of producing an
alternating cur-
rent, as such cur-
rent causes a
constant vibra-
tion of the dia-
phragm, the
vibrations in-
creasing in in-
tensity with an
increased flow
of current in

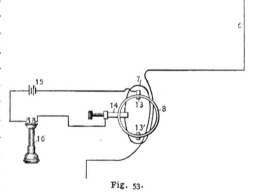

Fig. 53.

the circuit.   This increase in intensity of action with increased flow of current is characteristic of this form of
receiver.   In this it is sharply differentiated from such
devices as the coherer, which either give a strong indication or do not give any.   This characteristic is advantageous in that if the signal sent — say a dot — be too weak
to give an action of the full intensity, it may still in most
cases be read and not missed entirely, which is of value in
sending code-messages."

The Code-Message Trouble. — The above allusion to "code-messages" was probably first suggested by a declaration of the ocean cable companies that the Marconi Company could not transmit code-messages,—an idea now prevalent among inventors competing with the Marconi Company. Why the transmission of dots should not be necessary in ordinary messages has not been made clear; nor why there should be obstacles to the passage of code-messages which are sent by telegraphic signals exactly like other messages.

Mr. Fessenden's description of Fig. 53 includes the alternate use of a telegraphic sounder as a recording instrument in place of the telephone (16) shown; but it is hardly possible that a sounder in such position can have been successfully employed in practice.

Marconi's Opinion of Non-Tapping Coherers. — In a paper read before the Royal Institution of London in

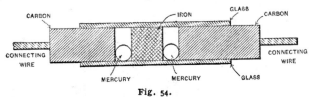

Fig. 54.

June, 1902, Signor Marconi says of non-tapping coherers, that they are not sufficiently reliable for commercial work; that under the influence of strong waves or of atmospheric discharges they cohere permanently; and that there is an unpleasant tendency to suspend action in the middle of a telegram; moreover, that as their resistance is continually varying, it is difficult to syntonize the circuits of which they form a part.

Italian Navy Radio-Receiver.—The radio-receiver adopted by the Italian navy, a result of the combined efforts of its experts, is a composite of the coherer and the microphone receiver.	It is used in connection with a circuit syntonized in the usual way by capacity and self-induction. The marked illustration, Fig. 54, seems sufficiently to describe it.

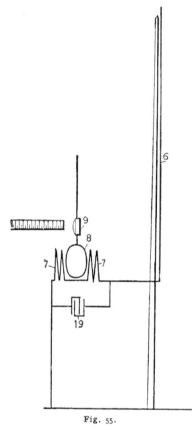

Fig. 55.

MAGNETIC—RADIO—
RECEIVERS.

In the class of magnetic-radio-receivers Mr. Fessenden has evolved three distinct types and Mr. Marconi one.

A Fessenden Magneto-Receiver. — Fig. 55 is an illustration of one of Mr. Fessenden's magneto-receivers, in which 7 and 7 represent field coils connected respectively to wave-gate 6 and to earth. 8 is an armature so suspended that the reaction of the current induced in 8 whenever the coils 7 are energized will cause 8 to move.	Such movement may be made observable by reflection of a beam of light from the mirror 9 upon a scale. The slight movement of the mirror is seen in the larger movement of the spot.

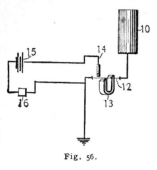

Fig. 56.

Another of Mr. Fessenden's devices is shown in Fig. 56, in which 10 is the wave-gate of a receiving station; 12 is a fine steel wire held under tension between the poles of magnet 13; 14 is a contact normally disconnected from wire 12 by the interaction of currents.

A Second Magneto-Receiver by Fessenden. — Fig. 57 is a diagrammatic representation from Mr. Fessenden's patent, No. 706,747, in which 10 is the antenna, 11 a coil having one terminal connected to the antenna 10, and the other terminal grounded. A telephone diaphragm 12, adapted to vibrate in unison with changes of current produced by waves radiated from the sending station, is suitably supported in operative relation to the coil 11; and the apparatus at the receiving station is tuned in harmony with the emitter of the sending station.

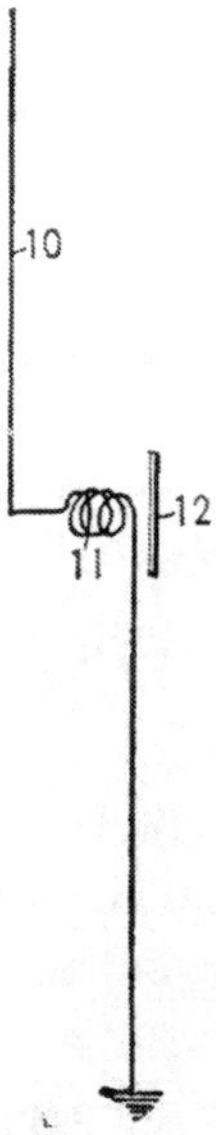

Marconi's Hysteresis Detector. —At this writing a description of the new Marconi receiver has been published, but no authorized illustration of it has been printed. In Fig. 58 an attempt is made to follow in diagram the

Fig. 57.

Marconi text.   The discovery upon which this new apparatus is based is the fact that hysteresis is decreased by the action of Hertzian waves.

Hysteresis Defined. — Whenever iron is subjected to changes in magnetic strength or magnetic polarity it generates and radiates heat.   This phenomenon is called "hysteresis," and the amount of heat dissipated as loss by reason of such changes is known as "hysteresis loss."

Changes of Polarity in Iron.   How Produced. — Differences in polarity may occur from movements of the iron itself, as when the armature of a dynamo revolves; or from the movements of a magnet, as when a dynamo field is caused to move about a stationary armature; or from changes in the exciting cause, as when an alternating current is made to pulsate through a transformer.

Quantitative Effects. — Quantitatively, hysteresis effect depends upon the amount of iron under influence; upon the quality of the metal, wrought-iron or steel being more affected than soft iron; upon the density of magnetism in the iron; and upon the rapidity of the movements which cause the changes in magnetic direction or magnetic power.

Theory. — Theoretically, it has been explained that heat is generated by friction as the molecules of iron in magnetic action turn over and thus rub against one another.

Description of Marconi Magnetic Detector. — Referring to Fig. 58, upon a core C, which consists of fine iron wires, are wound one or two layers B of thin insulated copper wires. Over this winding B, is an insulating coating G; around the insulating envelope a bobbin F F; and upon the bobbin a winding of small insulated wires, D. The ends of the winding B are connected respectively to the antenna A and the earth at E; and the ends of the winding

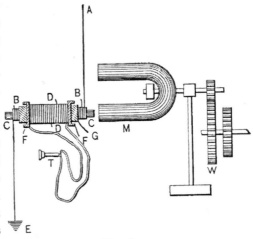

Fig. 58.

D to the telephone T. One face of the core C is presented to, and magnetized by, the magnet M. Upon being revolved by clock work, W, the movements of M cause constant reversals in the polarity of core C, and consequently a certain hysteresis effect is produced. Whenever this effect is modified by the influence of Hertzian waves, an audible record of such waves is made on the telephone receiver.

Practical Results From Marconi Magnetic Detector. — For some time the form of detector just described has been in successful operation over a distance of one hundred and nine miles of sea surface, and forty-three miles of high land, a total of one hundred and fifty-two miles. Marconi seems to think it is more sensitive and more reliable than a filings coherer.   Less electromotive force than with a coherer is required at the sending station ; its resistance is uniform ; and many of the precautions and delicate adjustments necessary where a coherer is used may be neglected with the hysteresis detector.

Coherer Organization Needed to Call. — So far, however, in order to "call," it has been necessary to use with the new receiver, a coherer, relay, and bell.   The only successful indicator of signals in connection with it is a telephone receiver.   If, as the tests seem to indicate, a visual record can be made and retained, Mr. Marconi thinks it will be possible to transmit several hundred words per minute.

A Wave-Responsive-Device by Fessenden. — It may be assumed that the result of Mr. Fessenden's labors for the United States Government, so far as wave-responsive-devices are concerned, is the subject of his patent No. 706,744, for which application was made on June 6, 1902, from the laboratory at Manteo, North Carolina.   In patent No. 706,745, the inventor claims that with the device so fully described in 706,744 "messages at the rate of thirty words per minute were sent and received over a distance of fifty miles, from Cape Hatteras to Roanoke Island, using at the sending end a spark only one thirty-second of an inch long." This form of radio-receiver from the Fessenden patents cannot be included in any of the four classifications just discussed.   The patentee himself describes it as "a current-actuated wave-responsive-device consisting of a conductor having a small heat capacity and arranged in a vacuum."

Description of Fessenden's Heat-Receiver. — Fig. 59 is a diagrammatic illustration reproduced from Mr. Fessenden's patent 706,744, in which 17 is a glass bulb. Into it are sealed two leading-in conductors of platinum wire, 16 16. 18 is a silver shell having at its top a glass brace 19, holding the wires 16 16. The platinum wires, except at the tip 14, are coated with silver. The tip 14 which is left uncoated is a minute part, being but a few hundred thousandths of an inch in length. Having small volume and capacity, the loop 14 is capable of being quickly raised in temperature an appreciable amount, and it is equally capable of quick cooling, thus producing rapid changes in electrical resistance.

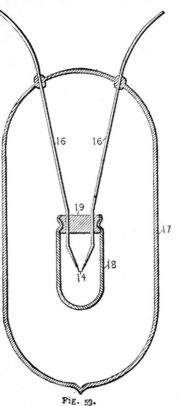

Fig. 59.

WAVE—GATES.

Marconi's Early Experiments in England. — In England, about August, 1896, Mr. Marconi transmitted signals overland a distance of two miles. No ground connection either at the sending or receiving stations was used.

Adoption of High Wire and Earth Terminal. — The next steps in the Marconi system were the adoption of an elevated terminal and an earth terminal. On May 11, 1897, Marconi, who was conducting experiments at Lavernock Point, England, failed of results. His receiving apparatus was set upon a cliff sixty feet above the level of the sea. Here was erected a pole ninety feet in height capped with a cylinder of zinc six feet long and three feet in diameter. An insulated copper wire was fastened to the cap, led down the pole, and from it made connection to one end of the coherer. The other end of the coherer was connected to a wire which was dropped down the cliff and dipped in the sea.

Communication Established by Better Earth and Longer Wave-Gate. — Both on that day and on the following, attempts at transmission were unsuccessful; but on May 13, the coherer and other receiving instruments having been carried to the bottom of the cliff, communication was at once established. The antenna by the change to the bottom of the cliff had been lengthened to one hundred and fifty feet. The earth connection had been strengthened by the elimination of such resistance as was furnished by sixty feet of wire.

Lodge's Early " Collecting Wire."— In Dr. Lodge's first patent, filed December 20, 1897, his wave-gate served for the reception of impulses, and was called by the inventor a " collecting wire." Presumably it was but a few feet in length. Quóting from that patent : " In some cases I find that any bare wire, or a connection to earth direct or through the system of gas or water pipes, will serve sufficiently well as a collector or as an assistance to the insulated collector."

Lodge Emitter. — Lodge devised a form of emitter [1] in which electricity was "supplied to a single conductor a suddenly or disruptively by a couple of positive and negative sparks from knobs b and c. A partial metallic inclosure d could be used to diminish waves in an undesired direction. There seems to have been no extension into space from the sphere a ; nor any switching communication between the sending and receiving sides of his apparatus.

A Supposed Law. — When virtue was found to exist in an elevated wire, Mr. Marconi made a number of experiments from which he deduced the law that the distance over which signals could be transmitted varied as the square of the height of the vertical conductors.

Lodge's Cones. — It was soon found, however, that no such law existed, and the attention of experts in wireless telegraphy was next given to devising wave-gates lower in height but greater in surface area. Dr. Lodge, in his United States patent filed February 1, 1898, says : " I prefer for the purpose of combining low resistance with

[1] Lodge patent, Appendix II.

great electrostatic capacity, cones, or triangles, or other such diverging surfaces, with the vertices adjoining and their larger areas spreading out into space." Manifestly such a construction as is shown in Fig. 25, Part I., would be especially weak to resist wind pressure, and so the inventor recommended a modification in the form of a roof, as illustrated in Fig. 21, Part I.

Marconi's Thick Copper Cable.— In a patent filed January 5, 1899, Marconi describes two wave-gates. The first was an insulated cable consisting of seven strands, each strand made of seven copper wires, each one millimeter in diameter, thus making the total diameter of the cable, the number of wires being forty-nine, nine millimeters, or thirty-six hundredths of an inch. This copper cable was suspended vertically from a height of one hundred and thirty feet.

Marconi's Iron Netting. — The second was a galvanized wire netting two feet broad and one hundred and thirty feet long, the top of the netting being about one hundred and ten feet from the ground.

Marconi's Observations on Wave-Gates in May, 1901.— In a paper before the Royal Society of Arts of London, May 15, 1901, Signor Marconi said : " The original elevated straight wire which was used as a transmitter was a very good radiator of electric waves ; but its electric oscillations died away with great rapidity, though very powerful while they lasted. If a radiator be used giving off much less energy at each vibration, but emitting a series of waves over an extended period, then it will only affect a resonator tuned to that particular frequency. It will take some time, measured in thousandths of a second, for the radiator to set up a swinging electric force in the receiver sufficient to break down the insulation of the coherer."

He further observed, in the same paper, that "early in 1900 the vertical wire was replaced by the zinc cylinder oscillators." The zinc cylinders are illustrated in Part II. as Fig. 37, and in the text accompanying that figure are described at length.

Fessenden's Wave-Gates of Low Resistance and Large Capacity. — In May, 1901, Mr. Fessenden, who had evidently been working along the same lines as Marconi, filed two patent applications whose subject matter chiefly concerned radiating conductors of low resistance and large capacity. Two of these are shown in Figs. 60 and 61. The inventor describes them as "sending conductors for electromagnetic waves," and says that they have a large capacity distributed with substantial uniformity over the radiating portion, and that this capacity is so adjusted that the waves radiated from the conductors have a low frequency. These conductors, it will be observed, differ from the Lodge cones in that, except for the enlargement in Fig. 61, they are uniform in figure.

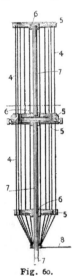

Fig. 60.

Mr. Fessenden says it has been held that the capacity of the upper portion of a conductor of uniform cross section is much lower than that of the middle or lower portion ; but that by actual measurements he has found this not to be the case, the upper portions having practically the same capacity as the lower. Further, he says, that when far from the ground the capacity of a conductor with respect to that ground is dependent not upon its distance from the earth, but upon its size and shape. Of the enlargement (17) in the middle of the sending conductor shown in Fig. 61, the inventor says :

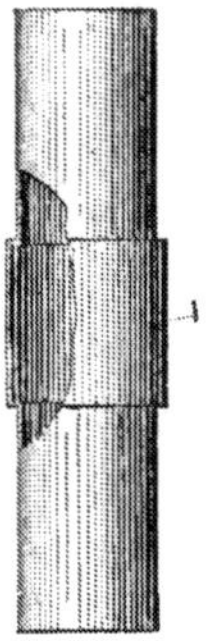

Fig. 61.

"The effect of locally increasing the superficial area of the sending-conductor, or of locally increasing the capacity by any other suitable means, is to produce two or more sets of waves of different periodicities, the periodicity of the first being dependent upon the electrical constants of the sending-conductor as whole, and the periodicity of the other depending upon the position and amount of localized increase of capacity, in the same way as by attaching a weight or spring to a piano wire between its extremities additional vibrations in the wire are created."

Fessenden's Wave-Gates of High Specific Inductive Capacity. — Figs. 62 and 63 are from the Fessenden patent 706,739. The first is a sectional elevation, and the second

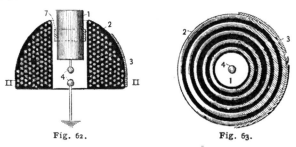

Fig. 62.   Fig. 63.

a plan of a sending conductor similar in configuration to that shown in Fig. 61, but now surrounded by a coil of wire, between the turns of which is supplied an insulating medium of high specific inductive capacity. " By this means," the patent declares, " it is possible to increase the capacity of the conductor without altering its height, and yet without altering the relation between the wave length and the medium and the length of the conductor. In other words, to obtain the same effect as is produced in air by increasing the height of the conductor "; or, again, "that all the functions or desirable results incident to the employment of a long high conductor can be attained by a relatively short low conductor."

In Figs. 62 and 63 reference number 1 indicates the radiating portion proper; 2 may consist of a coil of insulated iron wires of No. 40 Brown & Sharpe gauge. The wires in the coil are maintained under tension, the turns being spaced a distance apart approximately one-fourth the diameter of the wire. The spaces between the wires 2 may be filled with an insulating material of high specific inductive capacity,[1] such as rubber, indicated by a black mass in the figure; 3 is a reflecting plate formed of metal and arranged on the side of the conductor opposite that facing the direction in which the waves are to travel; 4 4 are spark knobs; 7 is an enlargement for a purpose similar to reference number 17 of Fig. 61. Of 7 the inventor says, it may be a band of conducting material, and that such a construction affords means for adjusting the capacity by adding or removing bands, or by changing their position along the conductor. The main advantage, and a matter of especial necessity to the Fessenden system, is that this device enables the operator to obtain long waves from a short conductor, thereby avoiding the expense involved in the erection of high masts.

[1] See p. 183.

Fessenden's Wave-Chute. — Another Fessenden invention is for a "wave-chute," called also an "artificial
ground." Of this device Fig. 64 is an elevation and Fig.
65 a plan. In those illustrations reference numbers 2

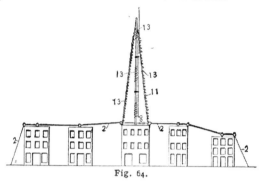

Fig. 64.

are longitudinal wires in the wave-chute; and 3, trans-
verse wires connecting together wires 2 ; 11 is a metallic
guy rope or chain for supporting the mast. In one of
his descriptions of the wave-chute the inventor says :

INVENTOR'S DESCRIPTION OF WAVE-CHUTE. — "I have found that it
is essential for the proper sending and receipt of these waves that the surface over which they are to travel should be highly conducting, more espe-

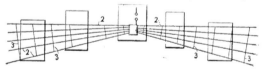

Fig. 65.

cially in the neighborhood of the point where the waves are generated. I
have found that this highly-conducting portion of the surface should preferably extend to at least a distance from the origin equal to a quarter wave
length of the wave in air, and in the direction toward the station or stations to which it is desired to send the waves. Where the sending-station
is in a city or similar place where the waves may be cut off by high build-
ings or high trees, this highly-conducting path should be extended still

farther, until it passes beyond the limits of the obstacle, and there the highly-conducting portion, which may be in the form of a strip of metal or other conductor, or of a number of wires, is connected to ground."

and, further, that "on rocky shores," as an instance, "salt spray sometimes dashes, rendering the ground surface near the station a conducting one which was previously an insulating one; and in such case an artificial ground makes the conditions constant in all weathers."

Preventing Absorption of Waves into Iron or Steel Guys. — "That it is preferable in such places to employ iron chains or iron wire ropes, and that such iron or steel guys would in general absorb waves rapidly," therefore he coats them and the mast with a non-magnetic film, such as zinc or lead, thus rendering their resistance to the currents produced by electromagnetic waves of the frequency used so low that there is little absorption. It is desirable that the guys be insulated from the ground, and "in order to render it certain that the natural period of the mast and guys is different from that of the electromagnetic waves, said mast and guys may be wrapped or encircled with one or more coils or turns (13) of iron strips, or wire, preferably insulated, thus increasing the inductance and natural period of the mast and guys, and permitting the employment of conducting material — e.g., iron or steel — in the mast and guys. As shown in Fig. 64, the coils or turns may be either formed locally, — i.e., extending a short distance along the mast or guys, — or such coils or turns may extend continuously along such parts.

"While the coating of the mast and guys with non-magnetic material need not necessarily be used with the coils or turns, it is preferred in most cases to both coat the mast and guys with non-magnetic material and also to employ the coils or turns of magnetic wire or strips, which may be formed of nickel or other magnetic material. No. 40 Brown & Sharpe gauge of wire is a size suitable for the purpose."

Probable Law or Wave-Propagation Through Space. — It seems natural and probable that the dissipation of energy in wave-propagation through space follows laws analogous to those that govern the conduction of electrical currents along wires, that the amount of loss is inversely proportional to the cross-sectional area of the conducting

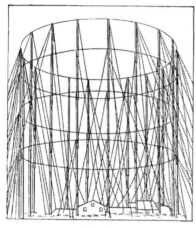

Fig. 66.

medium and to the square of the applied pressure. If etheric waves are radiated in straight lines, then the cross-sectional area of a wireless conductor is the product of the height and the mean horizontal periphery of the wave-gate. It is also true that the amount of energy which may be transferred from the surface of the sending conductor to the other is modified by the resistance to vibrations of the carrier which conveys those vibrations from the initial source of wave generation to the emitting surfaces.

The Marconi Wave-Gates at Poldhu and Glacé Bay. — Figs. 66, 67, and 68 are, respectively, illustrations of the

Marconi Company's wave-gates at Poldhu, England, and at Glacé Bay, Cape Breton. Fig. 68 carries out the idea of

Fig. 67.

Professor Lodge, referred to at some length in Part II., and also mentioned in the present part in connection with Lodge's wave-gate.

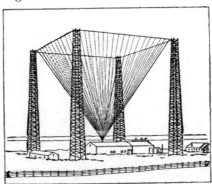

Fig. 68.

Cape Breton is an island and politically a part of the province of Nova Scotia. It is twelve miles from Sydney, and

separated from the main land by the Strait of Canso.
Each of the four towers, shown in the Glacé Bay picture,
are two hundred and fifteen feet high. They form a
square, each side of which is two hundred feet in length.
Between the eastern towers and the sea the ground is
absolutely bare of soil. The structures are composed of
strong steel timbers bolted together and firmly anchored
in foundations of cement concrete. At different heights
depend from the towers hundreds of steel guys (not shown
in the picture) are secured to the rocky surface of the
ledge from a few feet to fifty yards from their respective
bases.

SHIELDS.

A device peculiar to Wireless Telegraphy is the metal
shield used to protect the coherer from the strong waves
of a transmitter in close proximity at the same station.

Fig. 69 shows one of Dr. Lodge's devices, which he thus
describes :

COHERER SENSITIVE TO LOCAL AS WELL AS DISTANT OSCILLATIONS.
— " A coherer is sensitive not only to the desired impulse arriving from a

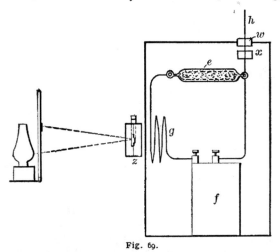

Fig. 69.

distance and conveyed to it by the collectors, but it is also liable to respond
to any local sparks or electric surgings in its neighborhood, especially to
oscillations in an adjacent emitter. It may be protected from all these by
complete inclosure in a flawless metallic box."

PROTECTION BY METALLIC COVERING. — " For the purpose of protecting the coherer from undesired disturbance, therefore, I inclose it (sometimes with all coils, wires, batteries, and the like connected to it) in a
metallic covering or case, as shown in Fig. 69, leaving only one or

more round holes or short tubes *w* for the collector terminal or terminals
to enter by, and for vision or other needful purpose requiring an aperture,
for through round holes of moderate size large electric waves do not
readily pass, whereas through chinks or long slits, no matter how infinitely
narrow, they can pass with ease. They likewise pass in by means of any
insulated wire which enters the box; but through any wire which is thoroughly joined to the metal wall of the box where it enters the waves cannot
pass."

DESCRIPTION OF FIG. 69. — " In the particular arrangement shown
in Fig. 69 a single terminal *h* is employed which is insulated from the casing by tube *w*, and is connected to one terminal only of the coherer. This
construction is effective and desirable in certain cases, and it is found that
the Hertzian waves pass in readily through the single wire. Hence it is
not absolutely necessary to remove the terminal *h* from its aperture when
it is not being used for the purpose of establishing communication and
enabling waves from the collector to enter the box and reach the coherer.

" The only part of the coherer or detector portion outside the box is
the index or needle mirror *z* of the telegraphic receiving instrument employed, which is acted upon and deflected by its coil *g* inside acting
magnetically through the metal wall.

" When the plan of withdrawing the terminals of the box is adopted, it
is sufficient to put the coherer above mentioned alone in the box."

Marconi's Shield. — Marconi's organization for shielding
his coherer is illustrated in Fig. 70.

His own description is as follows :

" When both instruments are employed at the same station, it is found
that the sensitive tube or sensitive imperfect contact is liable to injury by
its close proximity to the sparking appliance. In order to obviate this
objection, I inclose the receiver containing the sensitive tube or sensitive
imperfect contact in a box of metal having only a small opening into it,
and I employ the same conductor and earth-plate for both instruments.
The earth-plate is permanently connected to one terminal of the sparking
appliance and to the outside of the box. The insulated conductor can be
connected by a plug either to the other terminal of the sparking appliance
or to the other end of the imperfect contact.

"According to my present invention I inclose the receiver in a metallic
box A. One-twentieth of an inch is a suitable thickness for the metal.

The inside of the box is connected by a wire A' to the relay-circuit, and its outside by wires A^2 A^3 to one terminal of the telegraphic instrument h and earth E, respectively. The other branch of the relay-circuit is connected by a wire A^4, insulated from the box, to the other terminal of the instrument h.

"B is a coil on the wire A^4 and outside the box. It is protected from mechanical injury by a wooden case C; but this may be omitted. The coil B may contain about twenty yards of wire one seventy-fifth of an inch in diameter and have one hundred and twenty turns.

"The wire is insulated with gutta-percha D, which is covered with tin-foil F,

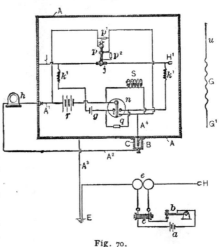

Fig. 70.

Fig. 71.

as shown in Fig. 71. The tin-foil is in electric connection with the box. The coil B prevents oscillations of the transmitter from reaching the coherer at the same station through the wire A^4. The aerial conductor u can be connected by a flexible conductor, plug G', and spring-contacts H and H' either to one of the balls e for transmitting or to one end of the tube j for receiving. The other end of the tube j is connected by a wire J to the inside of the box."

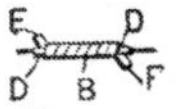

CONDENSERS, INDUCTANCE—COILS AND KEYS.

To round out this division of the work and to furnish means of ready reference, there is presented here a brief account of important principles and devices connected with Wireless Telegraphy, which, however, are neither novel nor peculiar to it.

Condensers. — When a source of electrical current is connected to a conductor, a long wire for instance, and that conductor is insulated both along its course and from a return wire or from the earth, it will become charged. Suppose instead of a long wire the conductor be a small sheet of tin-foil positively charged, and suppose another sheet of tin-foil negatively charged be placed near the first one, say, by gluing the two sheets upon opposite sides of a glass plate, then the amount of charge which may be spread upon the tin-foil sheets will be greatly increased. The total quantity of electricity which may thus be stored depends upon the area of the surfaces in the metal, upon the nearness to each other of the two oppositely charged sheets, which is to say the thinness of insulation between them, and also upon the composition of the insulating medium or "dielectric." Suppose two tin-foil sheets are joined together at their edges and interlaced with and insulated from two other sheets connected at the edges, then a diagrammatic expression would be as in Fig. 72, that diagram being the accepted symbol for a condenser.

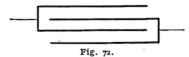

Fig. 72.

Multiplication of sheets increases, in direct proportion,

the capacity of the condenser for the storage of electricity. The amount stored is also more or less according to the "specific inductive capacity" of the insulating medium — the "dielectric." If the effect of dry air be taken as 1, that of rubber is equivalent to 3, of sulphur to 4, of mica to 7, and of glass to 9. For convenience and economy condensers are usually made of tin-foil plates separated by sheets of paraffined paper and sealed in a wood box.

Marconi's Condenser. — Marconi describes as follows the condenser used in connection with his earlier forms of apparatus for "tuning" the circuit. " It was composed of six tin-foil (or copper) plates connected to each terminal, each plate being 1.97 inches by 1.18 inches, the plates being insulated by paraffined paper, .067 inch thick. Its capacity measurement was one-fourth of one microfarad."

Tesla Condenser. — As has been shown already, the condenser plays a very important part in Tesla's wireless transmissions. In his sun motor patent shown in Fig. 15, Part I., he uses mica as a dielectric, and treats the condensers by a process of his own invention, consisting in inclosing the device in an air-tight receptacle, exhausting the air from the receptacle, introducing into a vessel containing the device an insulating material rendered fluid by heat, and when this material has permeated the interstices of the condenser subjecting the whole to pressure which is maintained until the material has cooled and solidified.

Improvements. — Other inventors have improved this process by so contriving the method of filling that the molten insulating material solidifies first in the interior

parts of the condenser and then on its edges.   Paraffin
wax is the principal ingredient of the insulating material
in these later inventions.

INDUCTANCE COILS.

Illustration of Lines of Magnetic Force. — Suppose a
piece of cardboard be held horizontally so that iron filings
will rest upon its surface, and that it be pierced through
its center by a vertical copper wire.   If the free ends of

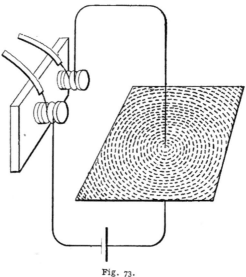

Fig. 73.

that wire above and below the card be connected to the
poles of a battery, the filings will arrange themselves in
radiating lines as in Fig. 73.   The influences which emanate from the wire are named magnetic lines of force, and
the area over which such influences are exerted is a magnetic field.

Induction Between Two Circuits. — If a second wire with its ends joined together, to make an endless loop, be brought into a magnetic field, there will be developed in this loop an electric current. If, while the two wires are in proximity, either the loop or the battery circuit be moved or the pressure in the battery circuit be varied, or the lines of force are passed across the loop, or the loop cuts them, or any electrical change is made, an electric circuit is set up in the loop.

Induction and Counter-Force in a Coil. — If a portion of a wire in a charged circuit be wound in a coil, the lines of force which may emanate from any one turn are cut by the wires of the other turns, and so a varying current may produce an inductive effect in that coil. The counter pressure thus created tends to stop the development of the flowing current, because the induced force is opposite in direction to the initial one; but if the flowing current be broken or weakened or strengthened, or in any way changed in direction or in force, then the secondary stream takes the same direction as the primary one, and, as both work together, there is a surge or impulse due to the sudden release of energy that has previously been bound.

One Coil is Placed Within Another. — It is the usual practice to place in the interior of a coil of one circuit turns of wire which are part of another. This arrangement secures the best results that may be had with coils alone, but a still greater effect is had by placing an iron core within the inner coil.[1]

[1] The analogy of inductive effect to the load upon a vibrating spring has been illustrated by Fig. 7, p. 29, Part I.

One of Marconi's Inductance Coils. — Mr. Marconi, describing an inductance, says :

Primary. — " The primary is wound upon a glass tube .635 cm. (about ¼ inch) in diameter. This primary winding consists of two parallel windings of two hundred turns each of copper wire .012 cm. in diameter (about .005 inch, or No. 36, B. & S. Gauge), the wire being insulated by a single covering of silk. The resistance of these two windings in parallel is about 3.1 ohms."

Secondary. — The secondary winding consists of 800 turns of a wire .005 cm. (.002 inch) in diameter, having a resistance of about 140 ohms, and wound either over or under the primary winding.

Another Marconi Winding. — Another Marconi inductance coil has the secondary wound directly upon a glass tube .3 inch diameter, the copper wire being .002 inch diameter with a single silk covering, and making three hundred and seventy-five turns about the tube with a resistance of seventy-nine ohms. Over this secondary is wound the primary of copper wire .005 inch in diameter with a single silk wrapping. Resistance seven and one-tenth ohms. Each of the four windings described consists of a single layer.

TRANSMITTING KEYS — KEYS IN SECONDARY CIRCUIT AND CONTACTS IN OIL.

In the initial American patent of Marconi, filed December, 1896, it is said that when working with large amounts of energy it is better to keep the primary circuit in constant operation and to interrupt the discharge of the secondary ; moreover, that in such cases the contacts of

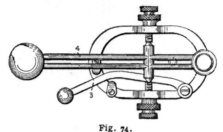

Fig. 74.

the key should be immersed in oil, lest, owing to the length of the spark, the current continue to pass after the contacts have been separated. In the DeForest system the key contacts are also made in oil.

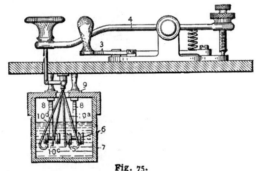

Fig. 75.

Fessenden Key-Contacts. — One of Mr. Fessenden's inventions in keys is illustrated by a plan view, Fig. 74, and sectional views, Fig. 75 and Fig. 76.

In this transmission it is intended to keep the generator in continuous operation, the manipulation of the key throwing the sending conductor out of tune with the receiving circuit of the distant station by short-circuiting more or less of the tuning device.

Referring to the figures, switch 3 is employed to render the generator inoperative while the apparatus is being used as a receiver ; 5 indicates one or more connected pairs of parallel wires to form a tuning grid ; 6 indicates movable contacts adapted to connect electrically the wires or conductors of each pair ; 7 is a box containing sufficient oil to

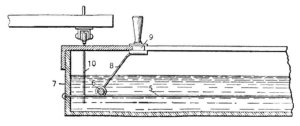

Fig. 76.

cover the wires to a depth of about one inch ; 8 are spring arms ; 9 are adjusting blocks mounted in arms in the cover of the box ; and 10, 10a, 10b, 10c, 10d are fingers arranged to be brought into successive contact with one or more of the wires of the grid, thus to shunt more or less of the capacity and self-inductance of the sending circuit.

MARCONI'S TRANSMITTING KEY AND LIGHTNING—GUARD.

In Fig. 77 is shown a key arrangement devised by Marconi for two objects, first, because the wave-gate is often charged with atmospheric electricity which, when it is shifted from the transmitting to the receiving circuit, is liable to impart to the operator and to the coherer an injurious shock ; and, second, to prevent the accidental

operation of the transmitter when the aerial conductor is
connected to receiver. The arm of the key is prolonged
beyond its pivot, and carries an insulated contact which is
permanently connected to the aerial conductor. Below
this contact on the base of the instrument is the terminal
of the receiver. The arm is so arranged that immediately

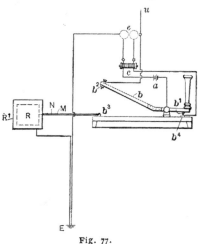

Fig. 77.

after its release by the operator, subsequent to the sending of a message, it turns about upon its pivot, bringing
the above-mentioned contact and terminal together, so
connecting the receiver with the aerial conductor.

In the drawing b' and $b4$ indicate the contacts of an
ordinary Morse key and a high insulating handle. The
extension arm b has an insulated contact $b2$. When the
key is released by the operator its longer arm falls by its
own weight, the contact $b2$ descending upon the contact $b3$.

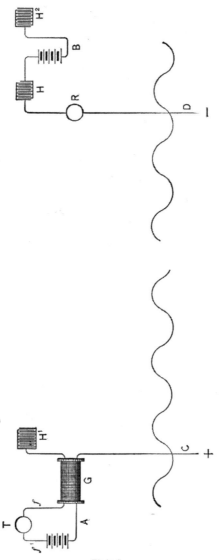

Plate I.

Reproduction of drawing accompanying United States Patent of Amos E. Dolbear,
No. 350,299, dated October 5, 1886.

[See p. 96.]

APPENDIX I.

UNITED STATES PATENT OFFICE.

AMOS EMERSON DOLBEAR, OF SOMERVILLE, MASSACHUSETTS,
ASSIGNOR, BY MESNE ASSIGNMENTS, TO THE DOLBEAR
ELECTRIC TELEPHONE COMPANY, OF NEW JERSEY.

MODE OF ELECTRIC COMMUNICATION.

Specification forming part of Letters Patent No. 350,299, dated
October 5, 1886.

Application filed March 24, 1882. Serial No. 56,264. (No model.)

To all whom it may concern :

Be it known that I, AMOS EMERSON DOLBEAR, of Somerville, in
the county of Middlesex and State of Massachusetts, have invented a
new Mode of Electric Communication, of which the following is
a full, clear, concise, and exact description, reference being had to
the accompanying diagram, forming a part hereof.

My invention relates to establishing electric communication between two or more places without the use of a wire or other like
conductor ; and it consists in connecting the transmitting-instrument
with a ground the potential of which is considerably above the
normal, and the receiving-instrument with a ground the potential
of which is considerably below the normal, the result being that an
impulse from the transmitter sufficient to cause the receiver to give
intelligible signals is transmitted through the earth without the need
of any circuit, such as has heretofore been deemed essential.

In the diagram, A represents one place (say Tufts College), and B
a distant place (say my residence).

C is a wire leading into the ground at A, and D a wire leading into
the ground at B.

G is a secondary coil, one convolution of which is cut, the ends
thus formed being connected with the poles of the battery f', which

has a number of cells sufficient to establish in the wire C, which is
connected with one terminal of the secondary coil G, an electromotive force of, say, one hundred volts. G in this instance also represents an induction-coil, T being a microphone-transmitter, f its
primary circuit, and f' its battery — that is, the battery f' not only
furnishes the current for the primary circuit, but also charges or elec-
trifies the secondary coil G and its terminals C and H'.

Now, if words be spoken in proximity to transmitter T, the vibration of its diaphragm will disturb the electric condition of the coil G,
and thereby vary the potential of the ground at A, and the variations
of the potential at A will cause corresponding variations of the
potential of the ground at B, and the receiver R at B will reproduce
the words spoken in proximity to transmitter T, as if the wires C D
were in contact or connected by a third wire. Electric communication may be thus established between points certainly more than half
a mile apart; but how much farther I cannot now say.

There are various well-known ways of electrifying the wire C to a
positive potential far in excess of a hundred volts, and the wire D to
a negative potential far in excess of a hundred volts.

In the diagram, H H' H² represent condensers, the condenser H'
being properly charged to give the desired effect. The condensers H
and H² are not essential, but are of some benefit; nor is the condenser H' essential when the secondary G is otherwise charged. I
prefer to charge all these condensers, as it is of prime importance
to keep the grounds of wires C and D oppositely electrified, and
while, as is obvious, this may be done by either the batteries or the
condensers, I prefer to use both.

The main difficulty in utilizing my invention on a large scale is
that when there are many spots corresponding to A and B signals
transmitted from any A will go to the nearest B, or to several B's,
depending upon proximity and other causes. One method of obviat-
ing this difficulty is to use a given A only during a certain assigned
time for communicating with a certain B, the particular B being
arranged to receive communications only during the assigned time.
Thus, if there were ten B's within a given area, then the first B might
be used for the first hour, the second B for the next hour, and so on,
and the first A for the first five minutes of the first hour, the second
A for the next five minutes, and so on, so that either one of the A's
might have free communication with the first B, each for its assigned
time during the first hour, and either A with the second B, each for
its assigned five minutes of the second hour, and so on.

In practice there will be of course both a receiver and transmitter at A and B, proper switches being used to bring either into use, as will be well understood without description.

I have spoken only of telephone-instruments, as these give the best results; but any electric instruments may be used capable of utilizing the currents passing through the earth from C to D, and the strength of such currents can be largely increased by increasing the positive potential of C and the negative potential of D. It will also be obvious that if the end of coil G (shown in the diagram as connected with one armature of condenser H') be grounded, and the end shown grounded be connected with the condenser, then C will be minus, and D must therefore be made plus.

What I claim is—

The art above described of communicating by electricity, consisting in first establishing a positive potential at one ground and a negative at another; secondly, varying the potential of one ground by means of transmitting apparatus, whereby the potential of the other ground is varied; and, lastly, operating receiving apparatus by the potential so varied, all substantially as described.

AMOS EMERSON DOLBEAR.

Witnesses:
G. B. MAYNADIER,
JOHN R. SNOW.

APPENDIX II.

UNITED STATES PATENT OFFICE.

OLIVER JOSEPH LODGE, OF LIVERPOOL, ENGLAND.

ELECTRIC TELEGRAPHY.

Specification forming part of Letters Patent No. 674,846, dated
May 21, 1901.

Application filed December 20, 1897. Serial No. 662,688. (No model.)

To all whom it may concern :

Be it known that I, OLIVER JOSEPH LODGE, a subject of the
Queen of Great Britain, residing at Liverpool, in the county of Lan-
caster, England, have invented certain new and useful Improvements
in Electric Telegraphy, of which the following is a specification.

My invention relates to electric telegraphy; and it consists mainly
in utilizing certain processes and combinations of apparatus whereby
I am enabled to demonstrate the presence of, and to indicate in a
receiving-circuit the reception of, what are known as "Hertzian
waves" emitted from any suitable apparatus at a distance from the
receiving-circuit and propagated through space. Thus after a succession of electrical surgings of predetermined duration have been
caused to emanate from the emitter in accordance with the Morse or
other code of telegraphic signaling the same are taken up in the
receiver-circuit and so rendered intelligible, and a telegraphic system
is thus obtained.

My invention relates, further, to certain improvements in connection with the emitting apparatus, and comprises the other improvements hereinafter more particularly described and claimed.

The annexed drawings, which are diagrammatic representations,
illustrate my invention.

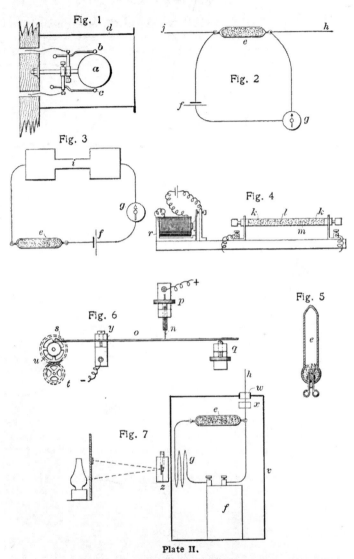

Plate II.

Reproduction of drawing accompanying United States Patent of Oliver Joseph Lodge,
No. 674,846, dated May 21, 1901.

Figure 1 shows the essential parts of one form of emitting appara tus. Fig. 2 illustrates one form, and Fig. 3 an alternative arrangement, of the apparatus and assembly of parts which constitute my receiving-circuit. Fig. 4 shows a form of "coherer," and likewise serves to illustrate a means for the automatic breaking down of the cohesion resulting from the reception of waves by the coherer, as hereinafter fully described. Fig. 5 illustrates an alternative form of coherer, and Fig. 6 a still further modified form thereof and an alternative means of breaking down cohesion. Fig. 7 shows the coherer and other parts incased within a metallic covering, as hereinafter described.

As emitter of the Hertzian waves for the purpose of this invention I may employ any known or suitable device in which a condenser or Leyden jar or other electric capacity consisting either of a pair of insulated plates or of a single plate and the earth is charged by an electrical machine (such as Wimshurst's), or a Ruhmkorff induction-coil, or a battery, or any other well-known means, to a high potential and then discharged suddenly with a spark between suitably arranged and prepared surfaces in air or in any medium, such as oil.

In Fig. 1 I have shown a form of emitter in which electricity is supplied to a single conductor a (shown as a sphere, but which may be of dumb-bell or any other shape) suddenly or disruptively by a couple of positive and negative sparks from knobs b and c and there left to oscillate and emit waves. A partial metallic inclosure d may be used to diminish waves in undesired directions. Both of these arrangements are my invention. The more usual plan hitherto has been to charge two conductors by a pair of leading-wires and let them spark into each other.

Referring now to Figs. 2 and 3, my receiving-circuit consists, essentially, of a coherer e, a battery f or other suitable source of electrical energy, and a telegraphic receiving instrument g, all in electrical connection, as shown. There is added to these latter a collecting-wire h, of any desired length, as shown in Fig. 2, or else a form of Hertzian resonator, as shown at i in Fig. 3, the function of either of which is to collect and to convey to the coherer the Hertzian waves produced at a distance, as aforesaid. In some cases I find that any bare wire or a connection to earth direct or through the system of gas or water-pipes, as shown at j in Fig. 2, will serve sufficiently well as a collector or as an assistance to the insulated collector.

The coherer consists, essentially, of an organism whose electrical resistance diminishes under the influence of Hertzian waves, but which returns to its former amount when the cohered condition brought about by the electrical influence is broken down by mechanical tremor.

One suitable form of coherer is illustrated in Fig. 4, which was introduced (for other purposes) by Branly previous to the year 1894. This arrangement consists of a pair of metallic points k, embedded in metallic grains or powder l within a glass tube m; but it will be understood that I may employ any other equivalent device. For example, I may seal the filings up in vacuum, as indicated in Fig. 5, which I have discovered increases and prolongs its sensitiveness, or I may, as illustrated in Fig. 6, use a coherer consisting of a needle-point n, resting lightly on a flat plate or spring o, fixed in a clamp y, the degree of pressure being obtained by the adjustment-screws p and q. On the arrival of Hertzian waves more complete contact or cohesion is set up between the particles of powder l or between the point n and spring or other light metallic contact o, and so allows more current from the battery f to flow through the telegraphic receiving instrument (indicated at g, Figs. 2, 3, and 7); but then before the coherer is again in a fit state to receive fresh impulses, the said cohesion must be destroyed. Now according to my invention I provide for this being effected by an automatic vibrator. This mechanical vibration may consist of a succession of jars or knocks or taps, which may be produced by electrical means, as in an electric trembling bell (see r in Fig. 4), or by clockwork (see Fig. 6). In the last-mentioned figure, s and t represent two wheels of a clockwork-train. Upon the arbor (or on a disk mounted thereon) of the wheel s is a series of serrations or the like u (shown exaggerated in the drawings), which as the wheel rotates effects the vibration of the lever or spring o either directly or indirectly through the stand. Such a tapper as is used in dentistry also serves very well for my purpose.

A coherer is sensitive not only to the desired impulse arriving from a distance and conveyed to it by the collectors, but it is also liable to respond to any local sparks or electric surgings in its neighborhood, especially to oscillations in an adjacent emitter. It may be protected from all these by complete inclosure in a flawless metallic box.

For the purpose of protecting the coherer from undesired disturbance, therefore, I inclose it (sometimes with all coils, wires, batteries, and the like connected to it) in a metallic covering or case, as shown at v in Fig. 7, leaving only one or more round holes or short tubes w for the collector terminal or terminals to enter by, and for vision or other needful purpose requiring an aperture, for through round holes of moderate size large electric waves do not readily pass, whereas through chinks or long slits, no matter how infinitely narrow, they can pass with ease. They likewise pass in by means of any insulated wire which enters the box; but through any wire which is thoroughly joined to the metal wall of the box where it enters the waves cannot pass.

In the particular arrangement shown in Fig. 7 a single terminal h is employed which is insulated from the casing by tube w and is connected to one terminal only of the coherer. This construction is effective and desirable in certain cases, and it is found that the Hertzian waves pass in as readily through the single wire, affecting the coherer in the same way as in the case of the earthed circuit through j in Fig. 2. Hence it is not absolutely necessary to remove the terminal h from its aperture when it is not being used for the purpose of establishing communication and enabling waves from the collector to enter the box and reach the coherer; for these same terminals h or j may when they are raised completely plug with metallic continuity, as shown at x, the small holes through which they can freely afterward be lowered.

The only part of the coherer or detector portion outside the box (shown in Fig. 7) is the index or needle mirror z of the telegraphic receiving instrument employed, which is acted upon and deflected by its coil g inside acting magnetically through the metal wall.

When the plan of withdrawing the terminals of the box is adopted, it is sufficient to put the coherer above mentioned alone in the box.

What I claim, and desire to secure by Letters Patent of the United States, is:

1. In a system of Hertzian-wave telegraphy, an emitter consisting of a single conducting body and means for suddenly and disruptively communicating opposite electric charges thereto, whereby oscillations are set up in said body, and waves are emitted, substantially as described.

2. In a system of Hertzian-wave telegraphy, an emitter comprising a single conductor supplied with opposite electricities by a pair of knobs connected to the terminals of a high-potential source.

3. In a system of Hertzian-wave telegraphy, the combination with an emitter, of a partial metallic inclosure serving to lessen the emission of Hertzian waves in undesired directions.

4. A coherer comprising a variable electrical contact sealed in vacuum.

5. In a receiver for Hertzian-wave signaling systems, the combina-

tion of the following instrumentalities: a coherer, a base or support upon which it is mounted, and a vibrator mounted in proximity to the coherer, and adapted to agitate its elements.

6. In the receiving-circuit of a system of Hertzian-wave telegraphy, the combination, with a coherer, of automatic means to successively break down the cohesion caused in said coherer by such Hertzian waves.

7. In combination, in the receiving-circuit of a system of Hertzian-wave telegraphy, a coherer, a battery, a telegraphic receiving instrument, and automatic means to successively break down the cohesion caused in said coherer by such Hertzian waves.

8. In combination, in the receiving-circuit of a system of Hertzian-wave telegraphy, a coherer, a battery, a telegraphic receiving instrument, automatic means to successively break down the cohesion caused in said coherer by such Hertzian waves, and means serving to collect and convey to the coherer Hertzian waves produced at a distance.

In testimony whereof I have hereunto subscribed my name.

OLIVER JOSEPH LODGE.

Witnesses:
    WM. PIERCE,
    WM. G. MURRAY.

REESE LIBRARY
OF THE
UNIVERSITY
OF
CALIFORNIA

APPENDIX III.

UNITED STATES PATENT OFFICE.

GUGLIELMO MARCONI, OF LONDON, ENGLAND, ASSIGNOR, BY MESNE
ASSIGNMENTS, TO MARCONI'S WIRELESS TELEGRAPH
COMPANY, LIMITED, OF ENGLAND.

TRANSMITTING ELECTRICAL IMPULSES AND SIGNALS AND APPARATUS THEREFOR.

Specifications forming part of Reissued Letters Patent No. 11,913,
dated June 4, 1901.

Original No. 586,193, dated July 13, 1897. Application for reissue filed April 1, 1901.
Serial No. 53,896.

To all whom it may concern :

Be it known that I, GUGLIELMO MARCONI, a subject of the King
of Italy, residing and having a post-office address at 18 Finch Lane,
Threadneedle Street, London, England, have invented certain new
and useful Improvements in Transmitting Electrical Impulses and
Signals and in Apparatus Therefor, of which the following is a
specification.

According to this invention electrical signals, actions, or manifestations are transmitted (through the air, earth, or water) by means of
oscillations of high frequency, such as have been called " Hertz
rays" or "Hertz oscillations." All line-wires may be dispensed
with. At the transmitting-station I preferably employ a Ruhmkorff
coil, having in its primary circuit a Morse key or other signaling
instrument and at its poles appliances for producing the desired
oscillations. The Ruhmkorff coil may, however, be replaced by any
other source of high-tension electricity. When working with large
amounts of energy, it is, however, better to keep the coil or trans-

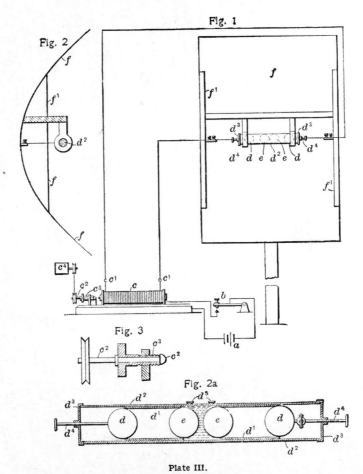

Plate III.

Reproduction of first sheet of drawings accompanying United States Patent of
Guglielmo Marconi, No. 11,913. (A reissue.)

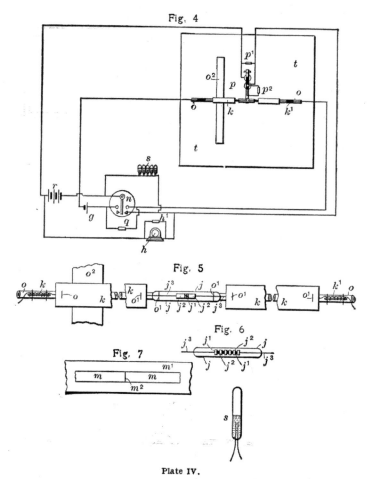

Fig. 4

Fig. 5

Fig. 6

Fig. 7

Plate IV.

Reproduction of second sheet of drawings accompanying United States Patent of Guglielmo Marconi, No. 11,913. (A reissue.)

Fig. 9

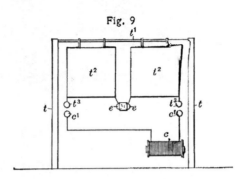

Fig. 10   Fig. 11

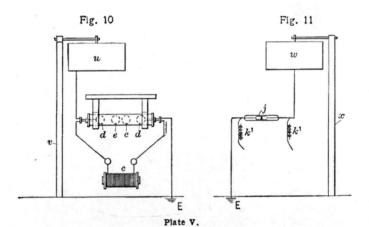

Plate V.

Reproduction of third sheet of drawings accompanying United States Patent of
Guglielmo Marconi, No. 11,913.   (A reissue.)

former constantly working for the time during which one is transmitting, and instead of interrupting the current of the primary
interrupting the discharge of the secondary. In this case the contacts of the key should be immersed in oil, as otherwise, owing to the
length of the spark, the current will continue to pass after the
contacts have been separated. At the receiving-station there is a
local-battery circuit containing any ordinary receiving instrument
and an appliance for closing the circuit, the latter being actuated by
the oscillations from the transmitting-station. When transmitting
through the air, and it is desired that the signal should only be sent
in one direction, I place the oscillation-producer at the transmitting-
station in the focus or focal line of a reflector directed to a receiving-station, and I place the circuit-closer at the receiving-station in a
similar reflector directed toward the transmitting-station. When
transmitting signals by the aid of earth connections, I connect one
end of the oscillation-producer and one end of the circuit-closer to
earth and the other ends to plates preferably electrically tuned with
each other in the air and insulated from earth.

Figure 1 is a diagrammatic front elevation of the instruments at
the transmitting-station when signaling through the air, and Fig. 2 is
a vertical section of the transmitter. Fig. 2a is a longitudinal section
of the oscillator to a larger scale. Fig. 3 shows a detail of the
trembler-break on a larger scale. Fig. 4 is a diagrammatic front
elevation of the instruments at the receiving-station. Fig. 5 is an
enlarged view of the receiver. Fig. 6 shows a modification of the
tube j. Fig. 7 shows the detector. Fig. 8 is a full-sized view of
the liquid resistance. Figs. 9 and 10 show modifications of the
arrangements at the transmitting-station. Fig. 11 shows a modification of the arrangements at the receiving-station.

Referring now to Fig. 1, a is a battery, and b an ordinary Morse
key closing the circuit through the primary of a Ruhmkorff coil c.
The terminals c' of the secondary circuit of the coil are connected to
two metallic balls dd, fixed by heat or otherwise at the ends of
tubes d' d', Fig. 2a, of insulating material, such as ebonite or vulcan-
ite. e e are similar balls fixed in the other ends of the tubes d'. The
tubes d' fit tightly in a similar tube d^2, having covers d^3, through
which pass rods d^4, connecting the balls d to the conductors. One
(or both) of the rods d^4 is connected to the ball d by a ball-and-
socket joint and has a screw-head upon it working in a nut in the
cover d^3. By turning the rod, therefore, the distance of the balls e
apart can be adjusted. d^5 represents holes in the tube d^2, through

which vaseline, oil, or like material is introduced into the space between the balls e.

The balls d and e are preferably of solid brass or copper, and the distance they should be apart depends on the quantity and electromotive force of the electricity employed, the effect increasing with the distance so long as the discharge passes freely. With a coil giving an ordinary eight-inch spark, the distance between e and e should, to assure good results, be from one twenty-fifth to one-thirtieth of an inch, and the distance between d and e about one and one-half inches. Other conditions being equal, the larger the balls the greater is the distance at which it is possible to communicate. I have generally used balls of solid brass of four inches diameter, giving oscillations of ten inches length of wave.

If a very powerful source of electricity giving a very long spark be employed, it is preferable to divide the spark-gap between the central balls of the oscillator into several smaller gaps in series. This may be done by introducing between the big balls smaller ones of about half an inch diameter, held in position by ebonite frames.

I find that the regularity and power of the discharge of an ordinary Ruhmkorff coil with a trembler-break on its primary is greatly improved by causing one of the contacts of the vibrating break to revolve rapidly. I do this preferably by having a revoluble central core c^2, Fig. 3, in an ordinary screw c^3, which is in communication with platinum contacts. I cause the said central core, with one of the platinum contacts attached to it, to revolve, preferably, by connecting it to a small electric motor c^4. This motor can be worked by the same circuit that works the coil, or, if necessary, by a separate circuit. The connections are not shown in the drawings. By this means the platinums are kept smooth, and any tendency to stick is removed. They last, also, much longer. At the receiving-station is a battery whose circuit includes an ordinary telegraphic instrument (or it may be a relay or other apparatus which is desired to work from a distance) and a circuit-closer.

In Fig. 4, g is the battery, and h a telegraphic instrument on the derived circuit of a relay n.

The appliance I employ as a circuit-closer is shown at Fig. 5, and consists of a glass tube j, containing metallic powder or grains of metal j', each end of the column of powder being connected to a metallic plate k of suitable length to cause the system to resonate electrically in unison with the electrical oscillations transmitted. The glass tube may be replaced in some places by one of gutta-percha or like material. Two short pieces j^2, preferably of thick silver wire of the same diameter as the internal diameter of the tube j, so as to fit tightly in it, are joined to two pieces of platinum wire j^3. The tube is closed and sealed onto the platinum wires j^3 at both ends.

Many metals can be employed for producing the powder or filings j^7; but I prefer to use a mixture of two or more different metals. I find hard nickel to be the best metal, and I prefer to add to the nickel filings, about ten per cent of hard-silver filings, which increase greatly the sensitiveness of the tube to electric oscillations. By increasing the proportion of silver powder or grains the sensitiveness of the tube also increases; but it is better for ordinary work not to have a tube of too great sensitiveness, as it might be influenced by atmospheric or other electricity. The sensitiveness can also be increased by adding a very small amount of mercury to the filings and mixing up until the mercury is absorbed.

The mercury must not be in such a quantity as to clot or cake the filings. An almost imperceptible globule is sufficient for a tube. Instead of mixing the mercury with the powder one can obtain the same effects by slightly amalgamating the inner surfaces of the plugs which are to be in contact with the filings. Very little mercury must be used, just sufficient to brighten the surface of the metallic plugs without showing any free globules. The size of the tube and the distance between the two metallic stops may vary under certain limits. The greater the space allowed for the powder the larger and coarser ought to be the filings or grains.

I prefer to make my sensitive tubes of the following size: The tube j is one and one-half inches long and one-tenth or one-twelfth of an inch in internal diameter. The length of the stops j^2 is about one-fifth of an inch, and the distance between the stops is about one-thirtieth of an inch. I find that the smaller the space between the stops in the tube the more sensitive it proves; but the space cannot under ordinary circumstances be excessively shortened without injuring the fidelity of the transmission.

The metallic powders ought not to be fine, but, rather, as coarse as can be produced by a large and rough file.

All the very fine powder ought to be removed by blowing or sifting.

The powder ought not to be compressed between the stops, but rather, loose, and in such a condition that when the tube is tapped the powder may be seen to move.

The tube must be sealed; but a vacuum inside it is not essential. A slight vacuum, however, results from having heated it while sealing it. Care must also be taken not to heat the tube too much in the center when sealing it, as it would oxidize the surfaces of the silver stops and also the powder, which would diminish its sensitiveness. I use in sealing the tubes a hydrogen and air flame. A vacuum is, however, desirable, and I have used one of about one one-thousandth of an atmosphere, obtained by a mercury-pump. It is also necessary for the powder or grains to be dry and free from grease or dirt, and the files used in producing the same ought to be frequently washed and dried, and used when warm.

If the tube has been well made, it should be sensitive to the induction of an ordinary electric bell when the same is working at one to two yards or more from the tube.

In order to keep the sensitive tube *j* in good working order, it is desirable, but not absolutely necessary, not to allow more than one milliampere to flow through it when active. If a stronger current is necessary, several tubes may be put in derivation between the tuned plates; but this arrangement is not quite as satisfactory as the single tube. It is necessary when using tubes of the type I have described not to insert in the circuit more than one coil of the Leclanche type, as a higher electromotive force than 1.5 volts is apt to pass a current through the tube even when no oscillations are transmitted. I can, however, construct tubes capable of working with a much higher electromotive force. Fig. 6 shows one of these tubes. In this tube instead of one space or gap filled with filings there are several spaces separated by sections of tight-fitting silver wire. A tube thus constructed, observing also the rules of construction of my tubes in general, will work satisfactorily if the electromotive force of the battery in circuit with the tube is equal to 1.2 volts multiplied by the number of gaps. With this tube, also, it is well not to allow a current of more than one milliampere to pass.

The tube *j* may be replaced by other forms of imperfect electrical contacts.

The plates *k* are of copper or aluminium or other metal, about half an inch or more broad, about one-fiftieth of an inch thick, and preferably of such a length as to be electrically tuned with the electric oscillations transmitted. The means I adopt for fixing the length of the plates is as follows: I stick a rectangular strip of tin-foil *m* (see Fig. 7) about twenty inches long (the length depends on the supposed length of wave that one is measuring), by means of a weak solution of gum, onto a glass plate m'. Then by means of a very sharp penknife or point, I cut across the middle of the tin-foil, leaving a mark of division m^2. If this detector is held in the proximity (four or five yards) and parallel with the axis of the oscillator in action it will show little sparks at m^2. If the length of the pieces of tin-foil approximates to the length of wave emitted from the oscillator, the spark will take place between them at a certain distance from the transmitter, which is a maximum when they are of suitable length. By shortening or lengthening the strips, therefore, it is easy to find the length most appropriate to the length of wave emitted by the oscillator. It is desirable to try this detector in the focus or focal line of the reflector. The length so found is the proper length for the plates k, or rather these should be about half an inch shorter on account of the length of the sensitive tube j, connected between them.

Instead of the tuned plates, k tubes or even wires may be employed.

f is a cylindrical parabolic reflector made by bending a metallic sheet, preferably of brass or copper, to form and fixing it to metallic or wooden ribs f'.

l is a cylindrical parabolic reflector similar to that used at the transmitting-station.

The reflectors applied to the receiver and transmitter ought to be, preferably, in length and opening, the double at least of the length of wave emitted from the oscillator.

It is slightly advantageous for the focal distance of the reflector at the receiving-station to be equal to one-fourth or three-fourths of the wave length of the oscillation transmitted.

I have hitherto only mentioned the use of cylindrical reflectors; but it is also possible to use ordinary concave reflectors, preferably parabolic, such as are used for projectors.

It is not essential to have a reflector at the transmitters and receivers; but in their absence the distance at which one can communicate is much smaller.

When no oscillations are sent from the transmitting-station, the tube j does not conduct the current and the local-battery circuit is broken; but when the powder or tube is influenced by the electrical oscillations from the transmitter it conducts and closes the circuit. I find, however, that when once started the powder in the tube continues to conduct even when the oscillations from the transmitter have ceased; but if it be shaken or tapped the circuit is broken. A tube well prepared will instantly interrupt the current passing through it at the slightest tap, provided it is inserted in a circuit in which there is little self-induction and small electromotive force, such as a single cell, and where the effects of self-induction have been removed by one of the methods which I will presently describe.

The two plates k communicate with the local circuit through two very small coils k', which I will call "choking-coils," formed by winding a few inches of very thin and insulated copper wire around a bit of iron wire about an inch and a half long. The object of these choking-coils is to prevent the high-frequency oscillation induced across these plates by the transmitter from dissipating itself by running along the local-battery wires, which might weaken its effect on the sensitive tube j. These choking-coils may, however, be sometimes replaced by simple thin wires. They may also be connected directly to the tube j. The local circuit in which the sensitive tube j is inserted, contains a sensitive relay n, preferably wound to a resistance of about twelve hundred ohms. This resistance need not be necessarily that of the relay, but may be the sum of the resistance of the relay and another additional resistance. The relay ought to be one possessing small self-induction.

The plates k, tube j, and coils k' are fastened by means of wire stitches o' to a thin glass tube o, preferably not longer than twelve inches, firmly fixed at one end to a strong piece of timber o^2. This may be done by means of wood or ebonite grasping-screws.

I do the tapping automatically by the current started by the tube, employing a trembler p on the circuit of the relay n similar in construction to that of an electric bell, but having a shorter arm. This vibrator must be carefully adjusted. Preferably the blows should be directed slightly upward to prevent the filings from getting caked. In place of tapping the tube, the powder can be disturbed by slightly moving outward and inward one or both of the stops j^2, the trembler being replaced by a small electromagnet (or magnets) whose armature is connected to the stop.

I ordinarily work the telegraphic receiver h (or other instruments) by a derivation, as shown, from the circuit which works the trembler p. They can also, however, be worked in series with the trembler. When working ordinary sounders or Morse apparatus, a special adjustment of the same is sometimes needed to enable one to obtain dots and dashes. Sometimes it is necessary to work the telegraphic instruments or relays from the back stops of the first relay, as is done in some systems of multiple telegraphy. Such adjustments are known to telegraphic experts.

By means of a tube with multiple gaps it is possible to work the trembler and also the signaling or other apparatus direct on the circuit which contains the tube ; but I prefer, when possible, to work with the single-gap tube and the relay, as shown. With a sensitive and well-constructed trembler it is also possible to work the trembler with the single-gap tube in series with it without the relay.

In derivation on the terminals of the relay n is placed an ordinary platinoid resistance double-wound (or wound on the "bight," as it is sometimes termed) coil q of about four times the resistance of the relay, which prevents the self-induction of the winding of the relay from affecting the sensitive tube.

The circuit actuated by the relay contains an ordinary battery r of about twelve cells and the trembler p, the resistance of the winding of which should be about one thousand ohms, and the core ought preferably to be of soft iron, hollow and split lengthwise, like most electromagnets used in telegraph instruments. In series or derivation from this circuit is inserted the telegraphic or other apparatus h, which one may desire to work. It is desirable that this instrument or apparatus, if on a derivation, should have a resistance equal to the resistance of the trembler p. A platinoid resistance h' of about five times the resistance of the instrument is inserted in derivation across the terminals of the instrument and connected as close to the same as possible. In derivation across the terminals of the trembler p is placed another platinoid resistance p', also of about five times the resistance of the trembler. A similar resistance p^2 is inserted in a circuit connecting the vibrating contacts of the trembler. In derivation across the terminals of the relay-circuit it is well to have a liquid resistance s, which is constituted of a series of tubes, one of which is shown full size in Fig. 8, filled with water acidulated with sulfuric acid. The number of these tubes in series across the said terminals ought to be about ten for a circuit of fifteen volts, so as to prevent, in consequence of their counter electromotive force, the current of the local battery from passing through them, but allowing the high-tension jerk of current generated at the opening of the circuit in the relay to pass smoothly across them without producing perturbing sparks at the movable contact of the relay. It is also necessary to insert a platinoid resistance in derivation on any apparatus one may be working on the local circuits. These resistances ought also to be inserted in derivation on the terminals of any resistance which may be apt to give self-induction.

I find it convenient when transmitting across long distances to make use of the transmitter shown in Fig. 9.

t t are two poles connected by a rope *t'*, to which are suspended, by means of insulating-suspenders, two metallic plates *f² f²*, preferably in the form of cylinders closed at the top, connected to the spheres *e* (in oil or other dielectric, as before) and to the other balls *f³* in proximity to the spheres *c'*, in communication with the coil or transformer *c*. The balls *f³* are not absolutely necessary, as the plates *f²* may be made to communicate with the coil transformer by means of thin insulated wires. The receiver I adopt with this transmitter is similar to it, except that the spheres *e* are replaced by the sensitive tube *j* and plates *k*, while the spheres *f³* are replaced by the choking-coils *k'*, in communication with the local circuit. It may be observed that, other conditions being equal, the larger the plates at the transmitter and receiver, and the higher they are from the earth, and to a certain extent the farther apart they are the greater is the distance at which correspondence is possible.

When transmitting with connections to the earth or water, I use a transmitter as shown in Fig. 10. I connect one of the spheres *d* to earth E, preferably by thick wire, and the other to a plate or elevated conductor *u*, carried by a pole *v* and insulated from earth; or the sphere *d* may be omitted and one of the spheres *e* be connected to earth, and the other to the plate or conductor *u*. At the receiving-station, Fig. 11, I connect one terminal of the sensitive tube *j* to earth E, also by a thick wire, and the other to a plate or elevated conductor *w*, preferably similar to *u*. The plate *w* may be suspended on a pole *x*, and must be insulated from earth. The larger the plates of the receiver and transmitter, and the higher from the earth the plates are carried the greater is the distance at which it is possible to communicate. When using the last-described apparatus, it is not necessary to have the two instruments in view of each other, as it is of no consequence if they are separated by mountains or other obstacles. At the receiver it is possible to pick up the oscillations from the earth or water without having the plate *w*. This may be done by connecting the terminals of the sensitive tube *j* to two earths preferably at a certain distance from each other and in a line with the direction from which the oscillations are coming. These connections must not be entirely conductive, but must contain a condenser of suitable capacity — say one square yard of surface. Balloons can also be used instead of plates on poles, provided they carry up a plate or are themselves made conductive by being covered with tin-foil. As the height to which they may be sent is great, the distance at which communication is possible becomes greatly multiplied. Kites may also be successfully employed, if made conductive by means of tin-foil.

The apparatus above described is so sensitive that it is essential either that the transmitters and receivers at each station should be at a considerable distance from each other or that they should be screened from each other by stout metal plates. It is sufficient to have all the telegraphic apparatus in a metal box and any exposed part of the circuit of the receiver inclosed in metallic tubes which are in electrical communication with the box. Of course the part of the apparatus which has to receive the radiation from the distant station must not be inclosed, but possibly screened from the local transmitter by means of metallic sheets. When working through the earth or water, the local receiver must be switched out of circuit when the transmitter is at work, and this may also be done when working through air.

The operation of my apparatus and system of communication or signals is as follows: The Ruhmkorff coil or other source of high tension electrically capable of producing Hertz oscillations being in circuit with a signaling instrument — such as a Morse key, for instance — the operator by closing the circuit in the way commonly employed for producing dots and dashes in ordinary telegraphy will cause the oscillator to produce either a short or a more prolonged electric discharge or spark or succession of sparks, and this will cause a corresponding short or more prolonged oscillation in the surrounding medium corresponding in duration to the short or longer electrical impulse which in ordinary telegraphy produces a dot or dash. Such oscillations of defined character will thereupon be propagated as such throughout the medium and will affect a properly-constructed instrument at a distant receiving-station. At such station the imperfect-contact instrument is in circuit with a relay, and when oscillations from the transmitting-station reach and act upon such imperfect contact its resistance is reduced, and the circuit is thereby closed during the continuance of the oscillation and for a length of time corresponding thereto. The closing of the relay-circuit causes the sounder or other signal apparatus to act in accordance with the particular oscillation received, and the oscillation also immediately starts the action of the shaking or tapping device, which so shakes the powder in the imperfect-contact instrument as to cause it to break circuit as soon as the oscillation ceases which has closed the circuit and produced a movement of the signaling instrument

corresponding thereto. I am therefore enabled to communicate signals telegraphically without wires by thus artificially forming oscillations at the transmitting-station into definite signals by means of a
signaling instrument and receiving and reading the same at a receiving-station by an imperfect-contact instrument, which when acted
upon by such defined oscillations operates, first, to close the circuit
in accordance with the received oscillation and produce a corresponding movement of the receiving instrument, relay, or sounder, and also
to operate a shaking device to automatically reopen the circuit
immediately after the reception of each oscillation, thereby preserv-
ing the results of its defined character in the action of the receiver.

All the details specified herein of construction of the sensitive
tube and its connections are desirable for great efficiency; but the
fundamental features of my system of transmission are not restricted
to such details.

I am aware that the sensitiveness of various apparatus, including
tubes containing filings, to more or less distant electrical disturbances
has been observed in a general way, and that it has also been proposed to disturb the conducting of such filings by various instrumentalities for shaking the tubes containing the same. I am also
aware that the use of tubes containing metallic powders of several
separate kinds has been described or suggested in connection with
certain experiments relating to so-called "coherers," but I am not
aware that the utility of a mixture of metallic powders has ever previous to my invention been ascertained and utilized for the purpose of
obtaining the required degree of sensitiveness in such an instrument.

I am aware of the publication of Professor Lodge of 1894, at London, England, entitled " *The Work of Hertz*" and the description
therein of various instruments in connection with manifestations of
Hertz oscillations. I am also aware of the papers by Professor Popoff
in the *Proceedings of the Physical and Chemical Society of Russia*
in 1895 or 1896; but in neither of these is there described a complete
system or mechanism capable of artificially producing Hertz oscillations and forming the same into and propagating them as definite
signals and capable of receiving and reproducing, telegraphically,
such definite signals; nor has any system been described, to my
knowledge, in which a Hertz oscillator at a transmitting-station and
an imperfect-contact instrument at a receiving-station are both
arranged with one terminal to earth and the other elevated or insulated ; nor am I aware that prior to my invention any practical form
of self-recovering imperfect-contact instrument has been described.

I believe that I am the first to discover and use any practical means for effective telegraphic transmission and intelligible reception of signals produced by artificially-formed Hertz oscillations.

What I claim is —

1. In an apparatus for communicating electrical signals by means of a producer of Hertz oscillations and a signaling instrument, the combination, in the receiver, of an imperfect electrical contact, a circuit through the contact, and a receiving instrument operated by the influence of such oscillations on said contact, substantially as and for the purpose described.

2. In an apparatus for communicating electrical signals by means of a producer of Hertz oscillations and a signaling instrument, the combination, in the receiver, of an imperfect electrical contact, a circuit through the contact, and means, controlled by said circuit, operating to shake the contact, substantially as and for the purpose described.

3. The combination, in an apparatus for communicating electrical signals, of a spark-producer at the transmitting-station, an earth connection to one end of the spark-producer, an insulated conductor connected to the other end, an imperfect electrical contact at the receiving-station, an earth connection to one end of the contact, an insulated conductor connected to the other end, and a circuit through the contact, substantially as and for the purpose described.

4. The combination, in an apparatus for communicating electrical signals, of a spark-producer at the transmitting-station, an earth connection to one end of the spark-producer, an insulated conductor connected to the other end, an imperfect electrical contact at the receiving-station, an earth connection to one end of the contact, an insulated conductor connected to the other end, a circuit through the contact, and means, controlled by the circuit, for shaking the contact, substantially as and for the purpose described.

5. The combination, in an apparatus for communicating electrical signals, of a spark-producer at the transmitting-station, an earth connection to one end of the spark-producer, an insulated conductor connected to the other end, an imperfect electrical contact at the receiving-station, choking-coils connected to each end of the contact, an earth connection to one end of the imperfect contact, an insulated conductor connected to the other end, and a circuit through the coils and contact, substantially as and for the purpose described.

6. The combination, in an apparatus for communicating electrical signals by means of a producer of Hertz oscillations and a

signaling instrument, an imperfect electrical contact at the receiving-station, choking-coils connected to the contact, a circuit through the coils and contact, and means, controlled by the circuit and operating to shake the contact, substantially as and for the purpose described.

7. The combination, in an apparatus for communicating electrical signals by means of a producer of Hertz oscillations and a signaling instrument, an imperfect electrical contact at the receiving-station, means, connected to each end of the contact, to prevent the oscillation from dissipating itself, a circuit through said means and contact, and means, controlled by the circuit and operating to shake the contact, substantially as and for the purpose described.

8. The combination, in an apparatus for communicating electrical signals, of a spark-producer at the transmitting-station, an earth connection to one end of the spark-producer, an insulated conductor connected to the other end, a tube containing metallic powder at the receiving-station, an earth connection to the powder and an insulated conductor also connected therewith, and a circuit through the powder, substantially as and for the purpose described.

9. The combination, in an apparatus for communicating electrical signals, of a spark-producer at the transmitting-station, an earth connection to one end of the spark-producer, an insulated conductor connected to the other end, a tube containing metallic powder, and an insulated conductor also connected therewith, a circuit through the powder and means, controlled by the circuit, for shaking the powder, substantially as and for the purpose described.

10. The combination, in an apparatus for communicating electrical signals, of a spark-producer at the transmitting-station, an earth connection to one end of the spark-producer, an insulated conductor connected to the other end, a tube containing metallic powder at the receiving-station, choking-coils connected to the powder, an earth connection to the powder and an insulated conductor also connected herewith, and a circuit through the coils and powder, substantially as and for the purpose described.

11. The combination, in an apparatus for communicating electrical signals, of a producer of Hertz oscillations, electrically connected with a signaling instrument at the transmitting-station, a tube containing metallic powder at the receiving-station, choking-coils connected to the powder, a circuit through the powder, and means, controlled by said circuit, for shaking the powder, substantially as and for the purpose described.

12. The combination, in an apparatus for communicating electrical signals, of a producer of Hertz oscillations, electrically connected with a signaling instrument at the transmitting-station, a tube containing metallic powder at the receiving-station, choking-coils and earth connection through condensers connected to the powder, and means, controlled by the circuit, for shaking the powder, substantially as and for the purpose described.

13. The combination, in an apparatus for communicating electrical signals, of a producer of Hertz oscillations, electrically connected with a signaling instrument at the transmitting-station, a tube containing metallic powder at the receiving-station, electrically-tuned devices connected to the powder, a circuit through the powder, and means, controlled by said circuit, for shaking the powder, substantially as and for the purpose described.

14. In a receiver for electrical oscillations, the combination of an imperfect electrical contact, tuned metallic plates connected to it, a circuit through the contact, and means, controlled by the circuit, for shaking the contact.

15. In a receiver for electrical oscillations, the combination of an imperfect electrical contact, choking-coils connected to the contact, a circuit through the coils and contact, and means, controlled by the circuit, for shaking the contact.

16. In a receiver for electrical oscillations, the combination of an imperfect electrical contact, tuned metallic plates and choking-coils connected to the contact, a circuit through the same, and means, controlled by the circuit, for shaking the contact.

17. In a receiver for electrical oscillations, the combination of a tube containing a mixture of metallic powders, a circuit through the same, and means, controlled by the circuit, for shaking the powder.

18. In a receiver for electrical oscillations, the combination of a tube containing a metallic powder or powders and mercury, a circuit through the same, and means, controlled by the circuit, for shaking the powder.

19. In a receiver for electrical oscillations, the combination of a tube, metallic plugs in the tube, metallic powder between the plugs, metallic plates connected to the plugs, choking-coils connected to the plugs, and a circuit through the coils, plugs, and powder.

20. In a receiver for electrical oscillations, the combination of a tube, metallic plugs in the tube, metallic powder between the plugs, metallic plates connected to the plugs, choking-coils connected to the

plugs, a circuit through the coils, plugs, and powder, and means, controlled by the circuit, for shaking the powder.

21. In a receiver for electrical oscillations, the combination of a tube, metallic plugs in the tube, a mixture of metallic powder and mercury between the plugs, choking-coils connected to the plugs, a circuit through the coils, plugs, and powder, and means, controlled by the circuit, for shaking the powder.

22. In a receiver for electrical oscillations, the combination of an imperfect electrical contact, choking-coils connected to the contact, a circuit through the coils and contact, a relay controlled by the circuit, and means, controlled by the relay, for shaking the contact.

23. In a receiver for electrical oscillations, the combination of an imperfect electrical contact, a circuit through the contact, an electric trembler shaking the contact, and means for preventing the self-induction of the trembler from affecting the contact.

24. The combination of a transmitter capable of producing electrical oscillations or rays of definite character at the will of the operator, and a receiver located at a distance and having a conductor tuned to respond to such oscillations, a variable-resistance medium in circuit with the conductor, whose resistance is altered by the received oscillations, means, controlled by the received oscillations, for restoring the resistance medium to its normal condition after the reception of such oscillations, and means for rendering the received oscillations manifest.

In witness whereof I have hereunto signed my name, at 18 Finch Lane, in the city of London, the 29th day of January, in the year 1901.

GUGLIELMO MARCONI.

In presence of —

SAMUEL FLOOD PAGE,
HUBERT WILLOUGHBY CORBY.

APPENDIX IV.

REPRESENTATIVE CLAIMS RELATING TO WIRELESS TRANSMISSION.

FROM THE UNITED STATES PATENTS OF NIKOLA TESLA[1] IN CHRONOLOGICAL ORDER OF FILING APPLICATIONS.

U. S. Patent No. 462,418, Nov. 3, 1891; filed Feb. 4, 1891.

1. The method of electrical conversion here described, which consists in discharging a condenser or conductor possessing capacity and maintaining a succession of intermittent or oscillating disruptive discharges of said conductor into a working circuit containing translating devices.

2. In a system of electrical conversion, the combination of a generator or source of electricity and a line or generating circuit containing a condenser or possessing capacity, and a working circuit operatively connected with the generating circuit through one or more air-gaps or breaks in the conducting medium, the electrical conditions being so adjusted that an intermittent or oscillating disruptive discharge from the generating into the working circuit will be maintained, as set forth.

U. S. Patent No. 454,622, June 23, 1891; filed April 25, 1891.

2. The method of producing an electric current for practical application, such as for electric lighting, which consists in generating or producing a current of enormous frequency and inducing by such current in a working circuit, or that to which the lighting devices are connected, a current of corresponding frequency and excessively high potential, as set forth.

3. The method of producing an electric current for practical

application, such as for electric lighting, which consists in charging a condenser by a given current, maintaining an intermittent or oscillatory discharge of said condenser through or into a primary circuit, and producing thereby in a secondary working-circuit in inductive relation to the primary very high potentials, as set forth.

U. S. Patent No. 568,176, Sept. 22, 1896; filed April 22, 1896.

1. The apparatus herein described for converting direct currents into currents of high frequency, comprising in combination a circuit of high self-induction, a circuit-controller adapted to make and break such circuit, a condenser into which the said circuit discharges when interrupted, and a transformer through the primary of which the condenser discharges as set forth.

2. The combination of a source of direct current and a circuit therefrom, choking-coils in said circuit, means for making and breaking the circuit through said coils, a condenser around the point of interruption in the said circuit and a transformer having its primary in circuit with the condenser as set forth.

3. The combination with a circuit of high self-induction and means for making and breaking the same, of a condenser around the point of interruption in the said circuit, and a transformer the primary of which is in the condenser-circuit as described.

U. S. Patent No. 568,178, Sept, 22, 1896; filed June 20, 1896.

1. The method of regulating the energy delivered by a system for the production of high-frequency currents and comprising a supply circuit, a condenser, a circuit through which the same discharges and means for controlling the charging of the condenser by the supply circuit and the discharging of the same, the said method consisting in varying the relations of the frequencies of the impulses in the circuits comprising the system, as set forth.

2. The method of regulating the energy delivered by a system for the production of high frequency currents comprising a supply-circuit of direct currents, a condenser adapted to be charged by the supply-circuit and to discharge through another circuit, the said method consisting in varying the frequency of the impulses of current from the supply circuit, as set forth.

3. The method of producing and regulating electric currents of high frequency which consists in directing impulses from a supply circuit into a charging circuit of high self-induction, charging a

condenser by the accumulated energy of such charging circuit, discharging the condenser through a circuit of low self-induction, raising the potential of the condenser discharge and varying the relations of the frequencies of the electrical impulses in the said circuits, as herein set forth.

U. S. Patent No. 568,179, Sept. 22, 1896; filed July 6, 1896.

1. The method herein described of producing electric currents of high frequency, which consists in generating an alternating current, charging a condenser thereby during determinate intervals of each wave of said current, and discharging the condenser through a circuit of low self-induction, as herein set forth.

4. The combination with a source of alternating current, a charging-circuit in which the energy of said current is stored, a circuit-controller adapted to interrupt the charging-circuit at determinate points in each wave, a condenser for receiving on the interruption of the charging-circuit, the energy accumulated therein, and a circuit into which the condenser discharges when connected therewith by the circuit-controller, as set forth.

U. S. Patent No. 568,180, Sept. 22, 1896; filed July 9, 1896.

1. The combination with a source of current, of a condenser adapted to be charged thereby, a circuit into which the condenser discharges in a series of rapid impulses, and a circuit controller for effecting the charging and discharge of said condenser, composed of conductors movable into and out of proximity with each other, whereby a spark may be maintained between them and the circuit closed thereby during determined intervals, as set forth.

U. S. Patent No. 577,670, Feb. 23, 1897; filed Sept. 3, 1896.

1. The combination with a source of electric energy, of a plurality of condensers and a discharge-circuit therefor, a motive device and a circuit-controller operated thereby and adapted to direct the energy of the source into the condensers and connect them with the discharge-circuit successively and in alternation, as set forth.

U. S. Patent No. 577,671, Feb. 23, 1897; filed Nov. 5, 1896.

1. The improvement in the manufacture of electrical devices such as condensers, which consists in inclosing the device in an

air-tight receptacle, exhausting the air from the receptacle, introducing into a vessel containing the device an insulating material
rendered fluid by heat, and then when said material has permeated the interstices of the said device, subjecting the whole to
pressure, and maintaining such pressure until the material has
cooled and solidified, as set forth.

U. S. Patent No. 645,576, March, 20, 1900; filed Sept. 2, 1897.

2. The method hereinbefore described of transmitting electrical
energy, which consists in producing at a generating station a very
high electrical pressure, conducting the current caused thereby to
earth and to a terminal at an elevation at which the atmosphere
serves as a conductor therefor, and collecting the current by a
second elevated terminal at a distance from the first.

5. The method hereinbefore described of transmitting electrical energy through the natural media, which consists in producing
between the earth and a generator-terminal elevated above the
same, at a generating station, electrical impulses of a sufficiently-
high electromotive force to render elevated air strata conducting,
causing thereby current impulses to pass, by conduction, through
the air strata, and collecting or receiving at a point distant from the
generating station, the energy of the current impulses by means of
a circuit synchronized with the impulses.

U. S. Patent No. 649,621, May 15, 1900; filed Sept. 2, 1897.

3. The combination with a transmitting instrument comprising
a transformer having its secondary connected to ground and to an
elevated terminal respectively, and means for impressing electrical oscillations upon its primary, of a receiving instrument comprising a transformer having its primary similarly connected to
ground and to an elevated terminal, and a translating device connected with its secondary, the capacity and inductance of the two
transformers having such values as to secure synchronism with
the impressed oscillations, as set forth.

5. The combination with a transmitting coil or conductor connected to ground and an elevated terminal respectively, and means
for producing electrical currents or oscillations in the same, of a
receiving coil or conductor similarly connected to ground and to
an elevated terminal and synchronized with the transmitting coil
or conductor, as set forth.

8. The combination with a transmitting coil or conductor connected to ground and to an elevated terminal respectively, and adapted to cause the propagation of currents or oscillations by conduction through the natural medium, of a receiving-circuit similarly connected to ground and to an elevated terminal, and of a capacity and inductance such that its period of vibration is the same as that of the transmitter, as set forth.

9. The transmitting or receiving circuit herein described, connected to ground and an elevated terminal respectively, and arranged in such manner that the elevated terminal is charged to the maximum potential developed in the circuit, as set forth.

10. The combination with a transmitting coil or conductor connected to ground and to an elevated terminal respectively of a receiving-circuit having a period of vibration corresponding to that of the transmitting circuit and similarly connected to ground and to an elevated terminal and so arranged that the elevated terminal is charged to the highest potential developed in the circuit, as set forth.

U. S. Patent No. 611,719, Oct. 4, 1898; filed Dec. 10, 1897.

2. The combination with a closed receptacle, of a circuit-controller contained therein and means for maintaining within said receptacle an inert atmosphere under pressure.

4. The combination with a circuit-controlling mechanism, one part or terminal of which is a conducting fluid, such as mercury, of a receptacle inclosing the same and means for maintaining an inert gas under pressure in the receptacle.

U. S. Patent No. 613,809, Nov. 8, 1898; filed July 1, 1898.

7. The combination with a source of electrical waves or disturbances and means for starting and stopping the same, of a vessel or vehicle, propelling and steering mechanism carried thereby, a circuit containing or connected with means for controlling the operation of said mechanism and adjusted or rendered sensitive to the waves or disturbances of the source, as set forth.

U. S. Patent No. 685,953, Nov. 5, 1901; filed June 24, 1899.

2. The method of transmitting and utilizing electrical energy herein described, which consists in producing electrical disturbances or effects capable of being transmitted to a distance through

the natural media, charging a condenser at a distant receiving
station with energy derived from such effects or disturbances, and
using for periods of time, predetermined as to succession and duration, the potential energy so obtained to operate a receiving device.

7. The method herein described of producing arbitrarily varied
or intermitted electrical disturbances or effects, transmitting such
disturbances or effects to a distant receiving station, establishing
thereby a flow of electrical energy in a circuit at such station, selecting or directing the impulses in said circuit so as to render
them suitable for charging a condenser, charging a condenser with
the impulses so selected or directed, and discharging the accumulated potential energy so obtained into, or through a receiving
device.

U. S. Patent No. 685,954, Nov. 5, 1901; filed Aug. 1, 1899.

4. The method hereinbefore described of utilizing effects or disturbances transmitted through the natural media, which consists
in controlling, by means of such effects or disturbances, the charging of an electrical condenser from an independent source, and
discharging the stored energy through a receiving circuit.

U. S. Patent No. 685,012, Oct. 22, 1901; filed March 21, 1900.

6. In a system for the transmission of energy, a series of transmitting and receiving circuits adapted to vibrate freely, in combination with means for artificially maintaining the same at a low
temperature, as set forth.

U. S. Patent 725,605, April 14, 1903; filed July 16, 1900.

1. In a system for the transmission of electrical energy, the
combination with means for producing two or more distinctive
kinds of disturbances or impulses, of receiving circuits, each tuned
to respond to the waves or impulses of one kind only, and a receiving device dependent for operation upon the conjoint action
of the several receiving circuits, as set forth.

7. The combination with a plurality of transmitter elements,
each adapted to produce a series of impulses or disturbances of a
distinctive character, and means for controlling and adjusting the
same, of a receiver having a plurality of sensitive circuits each
tuned so as to be affected by one of the series of impulses only,
and dependent for operation upon the conjoint action of all of said
circuits, as set forth.

8. The combination with a transmitter adapted to produce a series of electrical impulses or disturbances of distinctive character and in a given order of succession, of a receiving apparatus comprising tuned circuits responding to such impulses in a corresponding order, and dependent for operation upon the conjoint action of said elements, as set forth.

12. In a system for the transmission of electrical energy, the combination with a transmitting apparatus comprising a transformer and means for impressing upon the secondary element of the same oscillations or impulses of different character, of a receiving apparatus comprising a plurality of circuits each tuned to the impulses of one kind emitted by the secondary of the transmitting transformer, and a receiver dependent for operation upon the conjoint action of the receiving circuits, as set forth.

13. In a system for the transmission of electrical energy, the combination with a transmitting apparatus comprising a transformer and means for impressing upon the secondary elements of the same oscillations or impulses of different periodicities and in a given order of succession, of a receiving apparatus comprising a plurality of circuits each tuned to respond to the transmitted impulses of one period, and a receiver dependent for operation upon the conjoint action of the receiving circuits, as set forth.

16. In a system for the transmission of electrical energy, the combination with a transmitter adapted to produce electrical waves or oscillations varying in character in a predetermined order, of a receiving instrument responsive to said oscillations and dependent for operation upon the action thereof in a corresponding order, as set forth.

U. S. Patent 723,188, March 17, 1903; filed July 16, 1900.

1. The method of operating distant receivers which consists in producing and transmitting a plurality of kinds or classes of electrical impulses or disturbances, actuating by the impulses or disturbances of each kind or class one of a plurality of circuits tuned to respond to impulses of such kind or class and operating or controlling the operation of a receiver by the conjoint action of two or more of said circuits, as set forth.

3. The method of signaling which consists in producing a plurality of series of impulses or disturbances differing from each other in character and order of succession, exciting by the impulses of each series one of a plurality of receiving-circuits tuned

to respond exclusively thereto and controlling by the conjoint action of such circuits a local circuit, as set forth.

9. The improvement in the art of transmitting electrical energy which consists in operating or controlling a receiving mechanism by a series or group of electrical impulses of different periodicities and of a predetermined order of succession.

U. S. Patent No. 11,865; a reissue Oct. 23, 1900. Original filed Aug. 14, 1900.

1. The method of insulating electric conductors herein described which consists in imparting insulating properties to material surrounding or contiguous to the said conductors by the continued action thereon of a gaseous cooling agent, as set forth.

U. S. Patent No. 685,958, Nov. 5, 1901; filed March 21, 1901.

1. The method of utilizing radiant energy, which consists in charging one of the armatures of a condenser by rays or radiations, and the other armature by independent means, and discharging the condenser through a suitable receiver, as set forth.

INDEX.

CPSIA information can be obtained at www.ICGtesting.com
Printed in the USA
BVOW011056060712

294558BV00009B/49/P

9 781163 775011